Thank You
FOR
Sharing

Thank You FOR Sharing

A SUVIVOR'S GUIDE TO THE TWELVE-STEP RECOVERY WORLD

MARK GREY

PRIMIX
PUBLISHING
THE WRITE CHOICE

Primix Publishing
East Brunswick Office Evolution
1 Tower Center Boulevard, Ste 1510
East Brunswick, NJ 08816
www.primixpublishing.com
Phone: 1-800-538-5788

Published by Primix Publishing: 01/21/2025

ISBN: 979-8-89194-412-1(sc)
ISBN: 979-8-89194-413-8(e)

Library of Congress Control Number: 2025901629

This book is dedicated to Sandy, Glen, Mark W., my sponsor Ken, Robbie in Portland, Duane, Bubble Mike, Chuck, my mom, my two dads Phil and Chris, my uncle Arthur, my Higher Power, and to every twelve-step meeting I've ever been to and all the people I've met along the way.

I love you all!

Introduction

It's now January 16, 2024. On November 26, 2023, I picked up my twenty-two-year sobriety chip, and on January 2, I turned forty-five. I just found out early this morning that my good friend Glen, who managed San Francisco's world-famous twelve-step recovery club, the Dry Dock, passed away early this morning.

This news of Glen's passing has forced me to stop and take a hard look at what I'm doing with my life. The only thing I can come up with is that I feel very sad. I feel disconnected from everything. I feel cut off from my family, from friends, and even from myself. For example, I spoke with my Uncle Dan, my biological father's youngest brother, and tried calling my father to see how he's been doing the past couple of weeks. My father never picks up the phone, but this time he did.

Mark: "Chris, it's Mark."

Chris: "Mark. We just talked on Sunday."

Mark: "Dan has been trying to call you. Will you call him back and let him know you're okay? Dan's worried about you."

Chris: "I really don't want to talk to him."

Mark: "Is everything okay?"

Chris: "I just don't want to deal with the insanity."

Mark: "Oh, okay. But are you okay?"

Chris: "What do you care? If I say I'm not doing okay, what are you going to do about it?"

Mark: "Umm, I'm not sure."

Chris: "Exactly! You don't know. None of you know anything. None of you really care about me. You just call once in a while so you can feel good about yourself, but you don't really care. You can't help me!"

Mark: "Hey, Chris, I just want to make sure you're okay."

Chris: "Quit saying that. You always say that. But you don't care."

Mark: "Chris, I'm not sure what's going on here. I'm going to go. I don't know what to say."

Chris: "Okay, bye."

Click.

Man, I don't want this to be the way 2024 starts. For the past ten minutes, I've been re-reading that last sentence to myself, and it just hit me: every year, people get sick. Every year people die. Bad things happen. But good things happen too. Every year babies are introduced to the world, and people in love get married. My father is sick, and I'm not sure how much longer he's going to be alive. My good friend, Glen, passed away last night. But at the same time, some positive things have happened as well. Things that I don't even know about. And I don't need to know about those things for them to happen. I just need to know that good things happen. I can focus on my father being sick and Glen dying, or I can focus on the fact that I have three beautiful, healthy nieces who have their entire lives ahead of them. I want to have a positive outlook on life. I'm fully aware that the world is fucked up, but at the same time, the world is great. I just have the bad habit of focusing on the bad stuff. If I want 2024 to be a positive experience, I'm going to have to do something positive. I can't just expect things to be good without putting effort into the way I want life to be. I need to focus on doing something good.

The one positive thing I know I can do is tell stories. I love telling stories. I love listening to others tell stories, especially their own stories. So that's what I'm going to do. I'm going to go back to basics to bring something good to the world.

I plan to go to as many twelve-step recovery groups as I can attend this year and bring some of the stories I hear back to you. If you're new to recovery, you'll probably read some stories that will remind you of your own story. If you've been sober for thirty-five years, you might just find something that you've never heard before. And if you hit your ten-year sober birthday today and you're ashamed to tell someone that you're suffering from depression, I'm sure there will be a story in here that will match what you're going through. I hope there will be something for everyone in this book.

You're not alone.
You're loved.
We are all one.

When: 7:30 pm, 1.18.24
Where: 2900 24th Street, San Francisco
What: AA Meeting

There's a 7:30 pm AA meeting that I like to hit a couple of times a week in the Mission District. I like the mixture of people this meeting attracts. Some guys who stay at a local sober living house go to this meeting, a handful of Native American men and women always stop by, plus a lot of neighborhood people who live just a few blocks away come as well. This meeting is in an old building. The white paint is worn out, the light is a bit too bright, and the floors need to be redone, but I love this place. I like a little edge to my meetings. I'm not really into the preppy hipster meetings, even though I find myself at one of those meetings on occasion as well. A meeting is a meeting, but I do have my preferences.

A Gut Feeling

"My name is Mark, and I'm an alcoholic. I've had what I consider a typical alcoholic day today. I spent seven and a half hours in the Kaiser emergency room, and it was complete madness over there. It's fucking insane! And I've been there once before, like eight years ago, and it was just your average emergency room back then. But this time it was complete madness. Everything's changed in San Francisco. And I'm watching what's happening in the emergency room waiting room, and I felt like I shouldn't even be there. But I needed to be there. I was in serious physical pain, but I wasn't dying from a fentanyl overdose, and I'm not ninety years old suffering from a heart attack.

So this whole time I'm in the ER, I'm having this war in my head: *Should I go? Should I stay?* I've already spent three hours here, so I might as well stay. And this whole time I'm trying to be patient. Be patient. *Use the tools you have*, I say to myself. So I get my ribs X-rayed. And they're asking me why I'm in the ER, so I give them a whole list of things that are going on with me. The nurses and doctors tell me that I'm going to have to come back a few more times since they can only see me for one issue at a time. One nurse told me I could wait until 8:00 or 9:00 in the evening.

While waiting three hours for my name to be called by another nurse, another war raged inside my head. *What if this next doctor tells me I have colon cancer? What would I say? How would I react? Would I cry?* And then it hit me: I'm fucking all alone right now. I don't want to be like Matthew McConaughey in *Dallas Buyers Club* when he finds out he has AIDS. McConaughey's character was all alone when he was given that horrible news. One of my biggest fears is having to live with a painful disease that has no cure, all on my own.

I learned today that I can't be left alone in my head for hours at a time. Yes, I was in a jam-packed room full of people being carted around in hospital beds on wheels. I saw two guys slumped over in chairs, passed out, and foaming at the mouth and nose. I even saw a couple of nurses scream at a man to get out of the hospital because he wouldn't stop coughing on people and telling everyone he was going to give us all Covid. People were trying to sneak into the ER bathroom to do drugs. Kaiser has actually had to hire security guards for the ER bathroom. These poor guards have to stand next to the fucking bathroom door, ask people why they're going inside, and tell each person they have three minutes or they'll be escorted out. What the fuck?!? Even while this is all going on, I can still find a way to drown in my mind. *Am I going to die? When? How? Why?*

I found myself saying the Serenity Prayer over and over again, praying that God will help me not judge all these poor souls packed into this tiny ER waiting room. God, please help me not judge these people. I know these people are sick. There's so much sickness in this room. Please help us all.

Finally, I saw the next doctor at 5:02 pm. The doctor told me that my ribs were deeply bruised, but she said that I'd need to come back to the main Kaiser Hospital on Geary and go over some labs, take a bunch more blood and stool samples, and go from there. The entire time this doctor was talking to me, my head was racing. *Is this lady just gaslighting me, telling me everything's fine just so I'll leave and free up the chair I'm sitting in for the next poor bastard who's been waiting for eight hours?* I feel fucked up, and I know it's more than a bruised rib. It must be more than a bruised fucking rib.

I went back to the hospital the next day, and I found out that all this bullshit I'm going through is because I'm lactose intolerant. Lactose intolerant? Cheese can make me feel like I'm dying? Since when? These past two years of chronic diarrhea, constant gas, and my gut telling me to go fuck myself are all because I love Brie? A pale, creamy cheese from France is just as dangerous for me to consume as alcohol now. Fuck!

Look, guys, I know this has nothing to do with alcohol, and you probably want me to shut the fuck up right now, but I'm telling you this because, again, alcoholism is about the mind. It's not about alcohol. It's about not being able to shut your head up when you want to. It's about being powerless over so many situations in life. But again, I have the tools from working the steps and reading the books. I can talk to you about this shit. I can talk to my sponsor. There's a way out of the story I just told you. It's up to me to work with those tools I have and get out of the terrible situations I sometimes find myself in.

Thank you for listening to me.
Mark, Alcoholic.

When: 5:00 pm, 1.28.24
Where: West Pico Blvd. Los Angeles
What: ACA Meeting

I found myself in LA for a couple of days, mainly because I needed to get out of San Francisco. I always feel like I'm on a different planet when I'm in Los Angeles. I love LA people, but I hate having to be in a car all the time, and it always takes forever to get where I want to go. I don't drive, so I'm a slave to Lyft and Uber. But I will say this: Los Angeles has amazing twelve-step meetings. Some of the best meetings I've ever been to are in LA. I love the energy sober LA people have. People are friendly, dynamic, and open, which I like because I can be a bit of an introvert at meetings I don't know. I looked up the online meeting list for Los Angeles and found an ACA meeting on West Pico Blvd that was close enough. I spoke with a guy in his late twenties who had the best personality. Eventually, I just asked him if I could record him if he decided to share for my book. Timing is everything.

Love Is Complicated Sometimes

"Hi, guys. Dan, ACA. I had an interesting experience with my qualifier, my main qualifier. She started contacting me again around Thanksgiving/Christmas and said she was on her way and she was going to come stay with me with her son, who I raised since he was a baby. But that never happened. She never showed up. And we got engaged in conversation, and things were moving along, but she was texting me, and I requested that we talk on the phone so I could hear her voice and have a warm conversation. I like that. I need that to feel connected, instead of always having my face in my cellphone. Eventually she called me up and we finished our conversation. I thought everything was fine. But two days later, I got this scathing voicemail saying that she felt uncomfortable and that she was sick of my pressuring her all the time.

"I woke up to this voicemail. She sounded so angry. But I didn't know what she was talking about. How was I pressuring her? I wasn't forcing her to do anything. This voicemail sent me into a nosedive for an entire day. I called a couple of people in ACA, I called my sponsor, and I talked about it. That was the day before yesterday.

"Today, when I woke up, I remembered: oh, that's right, this woman suffers from mental illness. ACA! Or untreated ACA, I should say. And I remembered, I can't expect anything from this person. I forgot, again. I assumed that since things were going so well between us, she was all better. I assumed incorrectly. I was wrong. I thought she would be able to meet me halfway, but I was wrong. She can't. I thought that because I had been working all these programs and going to therapy, this woman would get better too. But that's not how it works. She has to work on herself, but she doesn't. Instead, when she gets scared, she yells at me and threatens me. So, when this happens, I stop talking to her and let time go by until she calms down a bit.

"And so today, I realized, I just can't respond to her when she behaves like this. Don't respond to the nasty voice messages or emails or texts. Just let those go. So, this is where I am today, and I hope things get better. Thanks again for listening to me."

When: 10:30 pm, 2.12.24
Where: Hollywood, California
What: AA Meeting

I liked the ACA meeting that I attended in Los Angeles so much that I decided to check out an online AA meeting that takes place in Hollywood every Monday at 10:30 pm. I immediately liked the people at this meeting. It almost felt like the *Hollywood Squares* TV show had a baby with New York's now-closed CBGB nightclub. Everybody had bright pink hair, tattoos, and T-shirts with insane prints on them. Was I in a John Waters film, or was this simply an AA meeting on Mars? Whatever it was, I was into it. After the meeting was over, I collected a couple of phone numbers for my next trip to Los Angeles. Now, here's Ron.

Covid, Meet Recovery

"Hi, guys. I'm Ron, and I'm an alcoholic. Welcome to Alcoholics Anonymous. Welcome to the new people, to the ones that identified and the ones who didn't. This is where the miracle happens, in Alcoholics Anonymous. If we don't work our program, if we don't get a sponsor, if we don't do everything we need to do, we're going to suffer. And boy, are you going to suffer. You know you see it every day when an alcoholic is in pain, but they refuse to do the steps. Nothing ever gets better when you're as sick as someone like me. And you know all that does is tell me that we're going to go back out eventually if we don't get into action and we get into excuses, into popularity, and all the other shit that distracts us from getting better.

"I know that I've been around here for a long time. I've seen a lot of people come and go. And I will tell you one thing: when you're not calling your sponsor, when you're not doing your Big Book work, when you're not reading the Big Book, when you're not making enough meetings, when you give, give, give too much in one area and not enough in another, you get lost. That's why we ask you to live in that triangle of recovery, unity, and service. I heard it early on: once you concentrate on one side of the triangle and not the others, one side gets shiny, and another side gets tarnished.

"Oh, and not to derail what I was just talking about, but I got Covid for the first time. Oh my God, I thought I was gonna die. It took everything I had just to log into this meeting. It's a bitch. I didn't think it was going to be this bad, but it's still affecting me. I've been sleeping twenty hours a day, and I don't do that. I'm an Aries, so I sleep three or four hours a night tops, then I'm up and running. Even if I don't go to sleep until 5:00 in the morning, I'm up at 7:00, and I go all day long. But this Covid really kicked my butt. Unfortunately, I gave it to my dad and my uncle, and now my uncle is in the hospital with Covid. I feel really bad, but all I can do is pray for him. Anyways, I know that's my time, but I want you all to know that I'm glad to be back in this meeting. I always feel so much better after hearing you all. Thanks again, everyone!"

When: 5:30 pm, 2.16.24
Where: Miami, Coconut Grove
What: AA Meeting

Welcome to Miami, everybody! It's Friday, it's gray and shit out, and the air is moody. I will be in Miami Beach for the next three days, but a friend of mine told me about an AA meeting in Coconut Grove. I kind of like Coconut Grove. It has this lush, laid-back, tropical vibe to it. I love the random peacocks roaming around and the chickens hanging out on Key West street corners. Coconut Grove, for me, kind of reminds me of SoCal's Venice Beach. Coconut Grove is just a bit more mature and has a preppy, middle-aged, cool gay guy vibe to it. So, maybe Coconut Grove isn't like Venice Beach after all.

I'm in Miami for a quick art festival this weekend, and my friend Julie told me I had to meet her. She offered to pay for my flight, so I'm here. Julie isn't sober by any means. She's the exact opposite of a sober living person, in fact, but she's one of my favorite people in the world. She asked me if she could come to the AA meeting with me, which I thought was kind of funny, but the more, the merrier, right? As soon as I met up with Julie, I knew she was on something.

She likes to take pills and mix them with alcohol on occasion, and she seemed to think it was a good idea to mix her Xanax with a little vodka before the meeting. During the meeting, Julie rested her head on my shoulder and dozed off for a bit. I prayed that she didn't start snoring or start talking to herself.

The meeting had a wild mix of people. Half the room was filled with women in their mid-sixties with heavy Southern accents, and the rest of the crowd seemed to be a mix of gay men in their early thirties from South America and beautiful Ukrainian women in their early twenties. And then there was me and Julie.

I really liked what everyone had to say at this meeting, but one woman seemed to have a calming effect on the room on this particular day, so I thought I would share what she had to say.

***

"Hi, everyone. My name is Nessa, and I'm an alcoholic. All I can say is wow! I love what everyone has had to say today. Manny, thank you for being of service today, and I love, love, loved what you said today. I saw you when you came into your first meeting, and I love how you express how your miracle is happening. You said, you know, what does that mean? Don't leave before the miracle happens. Yeah, miracles happen every day in sobriety. That's my experience. The joy of living. That's the true promise if you work. If you do the work in this program. There has to be action, you have a purpose, and then you follow through. Step three, you know, coming to have this power that I can rely on for everything in my life. You know, I never had that before I joined AA. That's why I was so full of fear. That's why I had to drink, right? And now today, no matter what. No matter what happens. And like what Art said, I have been riding a pink cloud for twenty-seven years too. Compared to what my life was like before this program, I do live in a pink cloud. And, yes, people have died, people get sick. I got sick, and one day I'll be gone. Life happens. But I still have the joy of living today because I chose to.

"There's nothing, and I mean nothing, like living sober for me. Step eleven. You know this didn't happen overnight. It had to come to me. I came to and I came to believe and I had to practice sitting quietly with myself and allow God to talk to me. I needed years to learn to trust, not only my higher power, not only myself but all of you. I had to learn to trust you. My sponsor used to say, oh, I believe in God, and I believe in this and that. But do you trust? Do you trust your God? Can you really let go? Can you let go and let God? Thank you so much, everyone, for letting me share what is on my heart today. I'll see you tomorrow."

Mark Webb
September 8, 1947 – March 6, 2024

Mark Webb, one of my best friends, died last week. I met Mark at a 10:00 pm AA meeting at the Dry Dock six years ago. I instantly realized that he was one of the most fascinating people I'd ever met, and he would become one of my very best friends. Mark was born in Milan, Italy, in 1947. His parents were Jewish Holocaust survivors, and his family moved to Boston when Mark was three years old. There's so much I could write about my friend Mark. The funny thing is that I was helping Mark write a book about his life. But before the book, there was my relationship with Mark.

Mark and I played mentor roles to each other. He and I worked the twelve steps of Adult Children of Alcoholics and Dysfunctional Families. For nine months, it seemed like Mark and I took turns having mini mental meltdowns over all the past trauma and life experiences we had gone through. We discovered that we had been shoving all our bad feelings deep down inside. Mark had issues with his mother, his ex-wife, and his two daughters. I had issues with my mother, grandmother, both fathers, and my brother. In my late teen years, I drank and used drugs to forget. Mark became one of the most powerful and wealthy lawyers in San Francisco, but he used pills and drank when he wasn't working. Mark got a divorce, lost touch with his daughters, and ended up in a basement apartment in San Francisco's Haight-Ashbury District. Mark lost the $8 million house in Tiburon and the vacation home in Montana. Even more importantly, Mark lost part of his soul for a while. Luckily, Mark decided to get sober. Mark found himself at the Dry Dock recovery club, and then I listened to Mark speak for three minutes about how he ended up in the ugly pink room at 10:00 pm on a random weekday.

I remember sharing right after Mark spoke and welcoming him to the Dry Dock. Immediately after the meeting ended, Mark grabbed my arm and asked me questions about how I got sober.

Mark: "Hey, buddy boy, how'd you do it?"

Me: "What, how'd I get sober?"

Mark: "Tell me all about it."

Me: "Right now?"

Mark: "Do you have anything better to do?"

Me: "Okay."

Mark and I chatted for maybe fifteen minutes, and then he told me he had to go but wanted to do lunch soon. He told me we were going to be friends. And so we became friends. For the first couple of years, I stopped by his basement apartment. We chatted about his daughters and how he was going to get them back. Mark wasn't so worried about relapsing on pills and booze. He never really talked about his personal drunkalogue. Mostly, Mark talked about his daughters, music, and art. Eventually, Mark started talking about his amazing father and his mother, who was deeply traumatized by her experience in World War II. For years, even after Mark and his family left Italy for Boston, Mark's mother was convinced that the Nazis were going to come to America and take Mark from her. On the other hand, everything Mark's father touched turned to gold. From what Mark told me over the years, his father was a genius with an electric personality. He became a well-known tap dancer, spoke at least four languages fluently, was a musician, a painter, and a very successful businessman. Mark became a lot like his father. Mark excelled in school, graduated first in his class at Harvard Law, became a painter, and produced a few small plays on the side. There wasn't much that Mark couldn't do.

Mark was one of my heroes. The funny thing is that every time I hung out with Mark, he always told me that I was his hero. I never understood why. Mark read all my books and showered me with compliments.

Mark: "Nobody speaks the truth like you do, Mark. Nobody. You know how to do something that so few people know how to do."

Me: "Thanks, Mark."

Mark: "Don't thank me. Just keep writing. You can never stop writing. Promise me you'll never stop writing."

Me: "I promise, Mark."

Mark: "Good!"

Mark was always one of my top cheerleaders. Mark also forced me to get out of the city with him. I don't have a car, but Mark liked taking long drives. We'd go to Napa for the day and talk about beautiful women and classical music. Mark always wore his French beret hat, a long scarf, and a trench coat wherever we went. Mark always looked like he was living in 1950s Paris. He was such a classy human being—well-spoken, creative, strong, and with a masculine mystique to him. The world we live in today doesn't allow for men like Mark to thrive. Today's modern politics, education systems, and, hell, even the food we eat are all turning men soft. And it's not because men want to be soft today. They have to be soft to sneak through the system. Men like Mark are dying off. Guys like Clint Eastwood, Arnold Schwarzenegger, and Bruce Willis are nothing more than symbols today. Clint is a thousand years old now, Arnold is right behind Clint, and Bruce has retired from acting because he can't remember what happened five minutes ago. Today's leading men aren't really men anymore. What it means to be a man has drastically changed. And I don't know if the change is good or bad. The hot shots in what is left of Hollywood are totally different from what I thought was cool back in 1987. Tom Holland, Timothée Chalamet, and Ashton Sanders are the world's new leading men, and they're nothing like Paul Newman, Jack Nicholson, or good ol' Clint Eastwood.

The world has changed, and I've reached an age when I'm uncomfortable regularly. I'm having a hard time adapting to what the world wants from me. Mark and I talked about this all the time. Mark said a few times how the world doesn't want you to be free anymore. Mark talked about how the old San Francisco made you feel like you could achieve anything, but today's San Francisco wants you to live in a cage. Maybe this is just one seventy-something-year-old man's observation of the world, or maybe he's right.

The last year of Mark's life seemed to be getting better and better. His law career was picking back up, and Mark was experiencing a kind of renaissance. During the holidays, Mark introduced me to a couple of women he was dating, and both of them were stunning. The only thing Mark couldn't seem to get a handle on was his relationship with his daughters. Every few weeks, Mark wanted advice on how to get his daughter to talk to him more. Mark loved his daughters so much, but he couldn't seem to get the kind of love he needed back from them. This is where Mark's sadness came from. Yes, Mark was a genius. Mark was a brilliant man who could achieve anything he wanted. But Mark was lonely. Mark was the kind of lonely person only another addict could understand. I understood Mark's loneliness. That's one of the main reasons why Mark clung to me.

Mark: "You get me, Mark. You understand what I'm feeling because you feel it too."

Me: "Yeah, I get it, Mark. It might never really go away 100%, but life is better when you have a few people in your life that get you."

Mark is one of the few people I have ever met who felt the kind of loneliness I feel and was brave enough to talk about it. I found Mark's ability to talk about his darker and more fragile side quite endearing. Mark wanted to let people in. Over the past four months, Mark, my editor, and I were slowly chipping away at Mark's biography. Mark had a creative obsession with *The Godfather* book and films and wanted to create a multigenerational piece about himself, his father, and his grandfather. Mark had plans to turn the book into a film. Mark's ideas always seemed to have a mind of their own. Everything he wanted to do always seemed to grow. I knew I was going to need a lot of help, so I reached out to my editor, Jeremy, another genius friend of mine. I knew Jeremy could give Mark what he wanted. My writing ability is much too limited to take on what Mark had envisioned. Within a couple of weeks, Jeremy and Mark were off and running. Things were starting to look great. It was starting to look like a book. And about a month ago, Mark reached out to me and said he needed me to write about his inner child. He wanted to fit his experience in ACA into his book and felt that I was the only person who could write it since we worked the twelve steps of Adult Children of Alcoholics and Dysfunctional Families together. In some ways,

I know more about Mark than most—if not all—people, and he wanted that in his book.

We were supposed to meet yesterday, March 10, 2024, at 2:00 pm. But I got a text at 8:16 pm the night before letting me know that Mark had passed away in his sleep and giving me the information about his funeral. When I was reading the information about Mark, his passing and the funeral, I left my body. It took a few minutes for this to sink in. My first reaction was anger. My selfish addict brain was pissed that Mark didn't let me know ahead of time that he was going to die in his sleep. How could another person know before me that Mark had died? Mark and I were best friends. Didn't that count for something? A few minutes later, I had to remind myself that I was nuts and needed to chill out.

At first, I tried to push away the feelings that were starting to creep into my mind. A heavy wave of darkness began to roll in. I was watching that Netflix show *Love Is Blind*, but I had to turn it off. I needed quiet. I got up, made my bed again, and just lay on my back and stared at the ceiling. Within a couple of minutes, the tears started to pour out. This one was going to hurt. I just prayed and cried. My good friend Mike called, and we talked for a while. I cried, and Mike went silent on the phone for a while.

Mike: "It's okay, man. I'll just be here on the phone."

Me: "Thanks, Mike. I'm sorry, but I have to do this for a minute."

Mike: "Don't be sorry man, this sucks."

After a while, I got a grip, and Mike and I told a couple of stories about Mark. We laughed. When Sunday rolled around, I made it over to Mark's funeral with a buddy of mine. The funeral was held at the Fernwood Cemetery in Mill Valley. Fernwood is a gorgeous place. It looks more like an upscale winery than a cemetery. Most of the people who attended Mark's funeral were wealthy lawyers, past clients, Mark's younger brother, his two daughters, his ex-wife, and his daughters' husbands. There were a handful of recovery people in the crowd as well. A rabbi led us all in the Kaddish mourner's prayer, and Mark's daughters said some nice words. Every time his daughters cried, I broke down and cried as well. It was an intense experience. Eventually, we all headed back to the main facility, ate some food, and took turns telling more stories about Mark. After half an hour of listening to people tell stories about Mark and what he was like back in the '80s, I left the event. I was supposed to speak at the podium, but I was exhausted, and I could tell that his family didn't want to hear the kind of stories I had to tell. They didn't want to hear about Mark and his recovery and how much he had grown over the years. Everyone wanted to talk about Mark the lawyer, and I didn't know that Mark. Out of respect for the room, I decided to skip my turn and just go home.

I know I'm supposed to be enlightened and say something spiritual like, "Mark is in a better place, and he's watching over all of us," but I miss Mark. I think it was too soon for Mark to go. I want Mark to be here. Friends don't grow on trees, and Mark was my friend. I'm going to miss you, Mark. Thank you for everything, and I love you.

When: 7:30 pm, 3.17.24
Where: Sunday Night Castro Speaker Discussion
What: AA Meeting

For the past couple of months, I've been going to more LGBTQ+ AA meetings. Yes, I'm a straight white male, and some people from this group may see me as the enemy, but for the most part, I haven't run into any issues. I've been going to San Francisco's Castro Country Club once or twice a week, and I recently started hitting up meetings at the Most Holy Redeemer Church, which is just a couple of blocks from the Castro Country Club.

I've noticed a few differences between gay and straight meetings. For one thing, gay meetings have a bit more pop to them than straight meetings. I've been to basic straight AA meetings all over the country, and for the most part, they're all basically the same. Yes, some are better than others. Some are a little safer than others, depending on the neighborhood the meeting is in, but in general, gay meetings have more energy. I like to be around people who are in decent shape and look like they work out and take care of themselves, and the simple truth is a lot of gay men like to hit the gym and look good. Straight men tend to let themselves go after thirty. People with energy who are in good shape are just more appealing to be around than people who are low energy and physically frumpy. Active, attractive people are more inspiring than those who aren't active and attractive. And look, I'm fully aware that I'm throwing a lot of generalizations around here, but I have to speak my truth. I simply like to be around attractive, energetic people who tell great stories.

Another thing I like about the gay meetings I've been checking out is that the meeting spaces themselves are much cleaner than the other meetings I've been going to that typically attract the breeder crowd. The Castro Country Club looks like a hip coffee shop now, and the meetings at the church I mentioned are also clean and tidy. The paint on the walls looks fresh, and the chairs are a little better than the chairs at the straight meetings. Overall, there's a higher level of hospitality at the gay meetings I've been going to. Clean walls, clean floors, laughter, easy banter between members, people with good hygiene, and the room doesn't have a slight scent of urine—what's not to love?

Sandy May was tonight's speaker. She's a mid-fifties transgender woman I've never met before, but the 120+ people in the room all seemed to already know her, and I got the feeling that tonight was going to be an amazing meeting. I didn't really know anyone, but luckily, I saw my good friend Jason, who goes to a lot of different types of meetings like I do. I ran over to Jason, gave him a high five, and we talked a little bit about the books we're both writing for a few minutes, and then the meeting started. I was really grooving on the energy in the room. There were so many conversations going on. A few guys were cutting up a big cake for after the meeting, and a couple more guys were making coffee and tea for everyone. As I was looking around, it hit me that I haven't been to a meeting like this in a few years. So many meetings have been crushed by the Covid lockdown, and most of those old meetings never came back. San Francisco AA was kicked in the gut by Covid. Places like the Dry Dock and the Gratitude Center are struggling to stay alive. The meetings I go to in the Mission District are also struggling. I just thought that all of San Francisco's AA meetings were in a death spiral, but I guess I was wrong. Some meeting spots are thriving and kicking ass, and it's great to see this. I feel so much better knowing this.

Just last night, I was talking to an old-timer with over thirty years of sobriety at the Dry Dock, and we were talking about how nervous we both were about the state of San Francisco and the Bay Area's AA meeting culture. Fewer and fewer people seem to be going to in-person AA meetings. So many meetings lack the kind of energy and camaraderie that we were used to just four years ago. Fewer people are volunteering their time at meetings. Nobody raises their hands to be the coffee person, the greeter, or the cleanup person anymore. Everybody just seems too burnt out these days. Last night, I had to admit that I haven't really been offering to sponsor new guys anymore. I've been hitting meetings every day, talking to a couple of people before and after the meeting, and talking to my sponsor once a week, but that's it. To someone who doesn't understand the recovery world, you might think what I listed off was enough, but if you're an addict in recovery, you know it takes more than just going to meetings and talking to a few people. It's more than just socializing. Recovery is about giving what you've gotten from AA and giving it to someone else. If you're not giving it away, then you could be fucked.

All the disappointment and yuckiness I've been feeling about the state of San Francisco's AA recovery culture lately went out the window tonight because I found a total gem of a meeting, and tonight's speaker was nothing short of amazing. Sandy May looked amazing, and I couldn't wait to hear what she had to say. Sandy May was dressed to the nines, in a black dress, big blonde hair, makeup done up, lots of cleavage, and high heels to boot.

SOMETIMES, LIFE IS A DRAG!

"Good evening, everybody, my name is Sandy May, and I'm an alcoholic. You know, back in the '60s, they didn't really look at mental health or anything like they do now. And I went through a lot of violence in my childhood. A few of the things I had to go through: my mother would try to suffocate me as an infant because I couldn't stop crying. The closest I can get to why this was happening, why I couldn't stop crying, was the trauma when you're adopted and taken away from your biological mother. So, my mother who adopted me couldn't stop me from crying. A lot of these answers I've had to come up with on my own because I never got a lot of closure with my mother.

"On Thanksgiving, she would make a big meal, and she would make sweet potatoes every year. And I hated sweet potatoes. I couldn't eat sweet potatoes. They would make me fucking gag. But she always had them on the plate. And so I just kind of saw that as punishment. I saw it as antagonistic punishment because that's the way my mother was. I tried different ways to get rid of the sweet potatoes. I would put them

27

in my napkin, and then I'd go to the toilet and flush 'em. I'd put the napkin in the toilet, and I'd cause a problem, and I'd get busted. So, I wasn't that good at being a rat back then. She would take me into the kitchen, sit me in a chair, and force-feed me sweet potatoes. But then I'd go back to the bathroom and throw all the sweet potatoes up. In the bathroom, there would be blood and sweet potatoes everywhere. I just went through this really violent thing with her.

"It got so bad with my mother that I just took off at twelve years old. It got to the point that she was going to accidentally kill me, or I was going to kill her. So I hit the road. I packed a hatbox. I do have to say that there was a gender crossroad from the beginning. My mother would always scream, 'I want a daughter! I didn't want three boys!' And every time my mother would say this, I would raise my hand. She'd look at me really mean, and maybe those were some of the things that got my mother to attack me. But before I took off, I stole all of her clothes and put them in my closet.

"Now, I didn't find out that I was transgender until I was fifty-six years old, but it's like this crossroad. So, I packed a hatbox, and I'm hitchhiking across the country, and the first vehicle that picks me up is this big white van. The van door opens, and all this pot smoke comes out, and a bong comes out. I grab the bong, and they take me, and I'm on my way. I don't know how long it took me to get to California. I joined a band and was the backup singer. I was on the streets. I was on the streets here in San Francisco, I was on the streets in New York, I was on the streets in Washington, DC. I was all over the country.

"I always wanted to tell this story where I was drunk driving, and I was in full drag in Washington, DC on a federal highway. I was in a blackout. I didn't know I was trying to kill the police officers that were after me. I tried running the police officers over with my car. My little brother was in the car with me. All I remember is that I was about to take an exit, and I came out of the blackout, and my little brother is screaming, 'Pull over!' And I told my little brother that I would pull over since there were police cars behind us. I didn't realize the police were after me. My tire was flat on GW Parkway. Sparks were flying. I don't know how many police cars there were. So they put me in jail. They had to call my father, who was a lieutenant colonel in the army, and he worked at the Pentagon, and he worked with Colin Powell, and it was 2:30 in the morning. And I had just gotten done with a Little Rascals Contest in Washington, DC. So once I got caught and was thrown into jail, I did what the law told me to do. I went to these classes, and everything was taken off my record.

"When I was traveling cross-country, I joined another band, and I fell in love with the band leader. I thought I had turned a corner, but one day I was at the house we lived in, and I went into our spare bedroom, and there was a pound of crystal meth—allegedly. In case anybody's out there. So, all of a sudden, surprise!

29

I'm in the drug business, and shortly after that, I'm a chef—allegedly. And we were doing deals where we were putting guns on the table, and everything started getting a bit wild. But I just have to say I was really bad at all this. Once I cut some drugs up with another cheaper drug that had rainbow colors in it. They bought it. You laugh now, but I swear to God, they bought it. And so, I was doing my last deal in Herndon, Virginia, and all of a sudden, a car pulled up to my right, and I had a gun on the steering wheel. I automatically put the car in reverse and hit a van that was behind me. They told me later that I almost ran over a police officer. Then I turned the wheel to the left, went over the median strip, and hit an unmarked car, and all I saw were guns. Then, all of a sudden, I saw like fifty police cars. They weren't in police uniforms, and they weren't in police cars. I didn't know they were the police at first. So, anyways, they put me in jail. But I always looked like a girl, and there was always girl shit going on, but I was so blonde I had no idea. I mean, if I ever had an idea, I think God kept it from me.

"So anyways, I go to jail, and then we're getting ready to go to court, and I think my bail was about $50,000. So we go in front of the judge, and the judge asked if I knew they were police officers. I told the judge that I had no idea. Then the judge asked if they showed any badges, and I said no. Then the judge said the case was dismissed. I was up for twenty-five years. I remember being in my lawyer's office, and I was fooling around, and my lawyer asked me if I knew I was facing twenty-five years in a state penitentiary? Now can you imagine what I would look like if I went to prison for twenty-five years? I have no clue. Probably more butch.

"As I'm traveling around, I'm on the road, and I'm in my mess, and I'm suffocating myself now with drugs and alcohol so I don't feel. I wanted someone to tell me how to do this life. I didn't know how to do this life. Not then. I had no fucking clue how to do this life. I wanted somebody to tell me how to live right. I kept asking people, and people would watch me, and they'd laugh. They'd watch me stumble over stuff and laugh. That's my memory as a kid. And then I found Alcoholics Anonymous.

"I walked in, and somebody said, come in, we're going to show you how to do this. At first, I didn't believe what anyone said. Nobody had ever offered to show me anything when I was a kid. When I first got sober, when I went to my first meeting, there was this guy named Barry. Barry was my first sponsor. And this was the first time that I ever felt God telling me what I needed to do. Barry becoming my sponsor was the first time I felt God pushing me in the right direction. And so, Barry took me on these sober retreats in the Santa Cruz Mountains, and I got to be ridiculous in front of people and be loved by people. You would drive up, and everyone would be at the front door, and you'd drive in and walk up to the door, and everyone would give you a standing ovation as you were coming in. There would be all these amazing speakers and food, and I did that for my first ten years of sobriety.

"I really love Alcoholics Anonymous. You know, if you look at my past, which you just heard, you can see that there's a big wreck back there, and there are bodies all over the place. And I have no problem conceding to myself that I'm an alcoholic. I know that with every fiber in my being. And I took the first step. And with the second and the third step, it's like, you know, being willing and then turning my life over to the rooms in the beginning because you were the only people who loved me. AA is so special to me. And then the fourth step. People are afraid to do this fourth step. To me, how I see the fourth step is that I've been going through my life, and I had all these manipulations. I had all this shit on how I was doing life, and it wasn't working. I didn't know that at the time. But the fourth step stripped all that stuff for me. All the bad stuff. All the shitty bad thoughts of being a rat and begging for food. Begging for love. Asking for money. I was a really bad prostitute. And I told my mother about it, and she tried to tell me I was a good one. But I was a really bad prostitute. I would get to the hotel, and I would get into the bed and just sit there with a scotch and look really angry. I swear to God. And they would leave the money on the dresser and leave the room. And I told my mom that I was the worst prostitute. And my mom would always tell me that I wasn't a bad prostitute. I was just a lazy one.

"So I had to learn how to do life. And once I'd gone through the fourth step and was able to get myself away from my thinking and to get myself away from the thought that I know anything. My sponsor… we would have meetings, and he would say something, and I would say, I know. And he would say something else, and I would say, I know. And he goes, listen, when you say, I know, to me, you're telling me to shut the fuck up. Can you change that to I understand, which keeps the door open? I've gotten so many gifts from this program. I've worked through all the stuff that happened when I was a kid. I can talk about it now and not become angry or depressed. Today my past is a tool that can help people.

"Whenever somebody says at the end of the meetings, 'Does anybody have a short share?' I always want to say, 'When the shit hits the fan, turn the fan off and pick up the phone and call one of us.' Because the thing is that AA, for me, is really kind of figuring out that I have issues—all kinds of issues—and how I can address them. How can I fix my life where I'm not stressed? How do I not get into the drama? One of the worst things that I went through—which is from what I understand, running rampant—is stories. We can tell ourselves stories, and we can get stuck in the story. We can get freaked out, and I can be close to a drink if I let a story get ahead of me. So, turning those stories over and being able to get on the phone and talk about what I'm constructing in my brain. Just by letting another person know what's going on in my head, I can get some sense of sanity, and I can let it go a little bit by a little bit. AA has taught me that shit's going to hit the fan, and it has.

"I found my birth family in recovery. My biological dad owned a cattle ranch up in Athens, Tennessee. And when I got there, he gave me a horse, a cow, and a bull. Jokingly, I looked at my Lincoln Town Car and let my dad know that I didn't think those animals were gonna fit. My dad really wanted me to stay in Athens, Tennessee. And, again, at this time, I was still hitchhiking all over the US, and I was really trying to find myself. I was trying to find where I belonged. And when I finally found my biological family, my dad and his wife, my stepmother, who was a year older than me. Don't forget, I was in Tennessee, so it's hard to figure it all out. My three sisters on my dad's side all died from drugs and alcohol by the age of thirty.

"I gotta say that when I met my father, I could have looked like anything. That was the first time I felt unconditional love. I worked the ranch. I actually became a real cattle rancher. I did all the stuff you do on a cattle ranch. I wanted to do everything. I needed to. We had to catch a cow, and the cow had all kinds of shit covering its body, and my dad said he had to clean up that cow, but I made sure I cleaned up the cow. I wanted every experience. I had enough sobriety that I didn't care what it looked like.

"Eventually, I put a house up on my dad's property. But the day before I had the electricity installed, my house caught on fire. Luckily, I had insurance on the house. But since I was in Tennessee, I thought it was the Klan that started the fire. I was driving a giant white Lincoln Town Car with a fluffy steering wheel in East Tennessee. And my cousin called me and asked why the hell I was out in the middle of Tennessee. She told me I had to get out of there. The AA meetings were interesting too. I said nothing. I just listened. So, the house caught fire, and it burned. Later, I found out that it was my stepmother. She burnt the house down because she didn't want me there. It took me a while to figure it out, but there's this thing, when there's property, and people are old, people will put their walls up so you don't get any money or property or whatever. My stepmother and the kids didn't want anything to do with me. So I got my money back from my house that burned down, and then I traveled some more. The one thing I'm happy about is that this all happened before transitioning was a thing. I mean, can you imagine if I walked up to my family back then the way I look today and introduced myself to those poor people? Hello, Dad, I'm your son.

But I have to say, my father would have accepted me 100%. He absolutely loved me. So, I buried my lover, my husband, who was my soul. My little brother died of AIDS. I was here in San Francisco when I lost two phone books' worth of friends to AIDS. One of the things that's important to know in AA is that life is gonna happen, and it's coming. And just because you're comfortable in the moment, it doesn't mean that shit's not gonna come down. I have to be ready for that. I started doing meetings here in San Francisco, and I lived in La Honda. But there are maybe only ten people in this room who were here when I started going to meetings in 1981. And a lot of people go out or disappear in some other way. But I decided a long time ago that I needed to really grab my seat in these rooms. I really wanted to be here. I have conquered a lot of things in my life. I decided to completely transition, and I didn't get any resistance from God, and it was all perfect. My life is so wonderful now. I have really great people in my life. I keep working this program because shit's gonna keep coming. I'm better at this program now, and I'm better at life now. I can let things go easier today, and I think the greatest thing that I got from AA is that I can be comfortable. Thank you very much for taking the time to listen to me tonight."

TAKING A BREAK FROM
ALL THIS SHIT

I've been binge-watching *The Conners*, the sitcom continuation series based on *Roseanne*, which has always had a special spot in my heart because she reminds me so much of my mother. As a kid, my family and I would watch *Roseanne* every Wednesday night. We'd eat ice cream and laugh our asses off. I basically grew up in a similar household as that show. My family is a bit white trash. There have been drug and alcohol issues throughout my mother's side of the family for years. One of my aunts is a lesbian. Even the furniture in the house I grew up in looked just like the furniture in the Conners' household. Roseanne's family was the funny version of the family I grew up in. The Conners always found a way to stay together, but in reality, what would really happen to a family like the Conners happened to my family. The drug and alcohol abuse caused my family to break apart, and it never came back together again.

My aunts and uncles, all my cousins, my parents, and my half-brother were all separated over the years.

We all did our best to create our own lives. We tried to build the kind of life we wanted when we were kids. Did any of us achieve the lives we wanted? Not really. But we did our best not to let this bother us. I think we all keep ourselves busy. Some of us got married and had kids, not necessarily in that order, but who's counting? My mother seems to have found a place in her mind that allows her to pretend her family is doing well. But are we? Maybe. Or maybe I'm too cynical to see what my mother sees.

I can only imagine what my stepfather really thinks. This man grew up in a pretty put-together family. Sure, they have their problems and dirty little secrets like all other families, but who knows what those secrets are? I know I don't. My stepfather must think my mother's side of the family is completely nuts. How couldn't he? I know I do.

This isn't coming from a nasty place of judgment like it did in the recent past. No, I genuinely believe that my family is collectively mentally ill. Most people who read this will think I must be coming from a negative place, but I'm not. If my family were all professional athletes, I'd tell people my family plays sports for a living. Or if I came from a family full of lawyers, I'd tell people everyone in my family practices law. But my family doesn't play sports for a living or sue people to make their living. My family is depressed, anxious, and just trying to make ends meet. Most of us will never be as successful as we'd like to be because our depression, anxiety, and general fear of life hold us back. Most of us will continue to hold menial jobs that don't pay very well. We will hopefully find a way to keep our health insurance and maybe take a trip to a city in the US every three or four years. But I could be wrong. I hope I am. For now, the picture I'm painting for you seems to be the world most of us will live in for the foreseeable future. For better or worse, in sickness and health, we seem to be married to the realities we've created for ourselves.

For years, I always felt I was separate from my family. I was destined for something different. Sometimes I still do, but as time creeps by, I'm not so sure anymore. So many people around me feel the need to tell me that I seem like I have my life put together. That I always seem to fall on my feet like some sly alley cat. Either I can't see what these people see, or they're simply lying to me. But what I'm describing to you is classic clinical depression. Depressed people don't see the bright side of life. They only see the dark parts of their pasts. I'm definitely guilty of this. My mother tells me to stop doing this. She tells me I'm successful. But who is my mother comparing me to? I know she's not comparing me to someone my age who went to Yale and got an amazing job right after graduating. I know she's not comparing me to a twenty-something Google employee making $140K a year managing some intangible group of ideas that I can't even begin to understand. I still don't understand how someone can make six figures a year managing multiple social media sites. I don't understand why that job is important and why it commands such an amazing salary. I don't understand AI, Instagram influencers, and I don't get why people are still talking about imaginary money. None of this shit is real. I think I need a break from all this.

You'd think it would be easy to turn all this off, but it's not. It's not just on my phone. These ideas are everywhere. I don't want anything to do with any of it, but it's almost to the point where it's not a choice. At least not in San Francisco. San Francisco insists that we drink this tech Kool-Aid. San Francisco wants us to chop off our tits and balls, dedicate ourselves to consuming the next big thing, and cut out anything or anyone that disagrees with these ideas. These are some dark times, but the sky is blue. It's so confusing sometimes. I'm not sure if someone living in a small town in Iowa can relate to what I'm talking about, but what I'm describing is happening where I live. In the Blue city I live in, stealing is legal, pedophiles are being somewhat celebrated, and an apple costs two bucks now. Shit is getting weird out here. I'm not sure if taking a break is even an option at this point. I'll let you know.

MY NEW DIGS

God, grant me the serenity to accept the things I cannot change, the courage to change the things I can, and the wisdom to know the difference.

I've been repeating the Serenity Prayer to myself a lot the past few days. I just moved into my new studio apartment a week ago. Everything was going great, or at least I thought it was. I manage the building I just moved to on Geary and Leavenworth. Geary Street is right on the fringe of Lower Nob Hill and the Tenderloin. I took the apartment because it will knock off about $500 off my rent every month. My goal is to move to Hawaii in a year. It's no secret that I'm a bit burned out on San Francisco. The homeless, the crime, the fentanyl, and of course all the wokester women with green and yellow hair and the feminist men who were brainwashed into loving them—I feel like I'm on Mars, and I'm not interested. So I found the cheapest place I could find through my work, and I took it. Everyone keeps asking me, "Dude, Mark, why did you move to Geary and Leavenworth?" I just smile and tell everyone that I have a plan.

Like I said, I thought everything was going well. But, on Monday, one of my supervisors told me that I have to move out of the building I just moved into, and they have to find me a different building ASAP.

Me: "What? Why? I just moved in. Do you know how much it costs to move in this city? My moving team was $600 alone. I don't want to pay for that again. What's the problem?"

Supervisor: "The San Francisco Tenants Union has said they don't want you in that building?"

Me: "What? Why?"

Supervisor: "They said that the last building you managed in the Tenderloin, you had a history of stealing tenants' packages and yelling at a few tenants that they represent."

Me: "What? That's crazy! I never stole packages or yelled at tenants. This is nuts! Who would say that?"

Supervisor: "I wasn't at the meeting, but this is what was said."

Me: "Who can I talk to about this? I didn't do any of those things. I don't want to move. There has to be something we can do."

Supervisor: "For now, all we can do is find you a new building. Sorry, man."

Click.

Powerless. This is the only word that comes to mind at the moment. There's nothing I can do about this situation right now. My HR manager will call me next Monday, and she will explain in more detail what is going on. All I want to do is get ahold of the person who makes these types of decisions and ask for proof. None of this makes sense, and I want answers. At the moment, I'm just guilty. I can't even defend myself. Who would say that I stole from other people? Who would take the time to create accusations like this? If I did these things and if I was reported for doing such things, why didn't the company I worked for at the time confront me? I never had any talk with managers or HR managers about yelling at tenants. Why is this all coming up now, two years since I stopped managing that building in the TL? The whole situation is ridiculous, and it's being managed by lazy people. This situation I'm going through is just one example proving that our entire society is falling apart. Lazy people who crave power are extremely dangerous.

Part of me wants to scream, but I know I've done nothing wrong. Getting hung up on all this corruption makes me part of the problem. I've given my side of the story. If I'm not granted the ability to smooth things over, then fuck it. This morning, I found out that my company has already found me another building to live in and manage. 810 Eddy is a better building in a slightly cleaner part of town. My apartment will be a little larger, so there are a couple of pluses right there. If San Francisco's Woke Nazi Tenant Protection Board needs to believe I'm the devil without ever meeting me, then so be it. Fuck 'em. I'll just keep working, writing, and saving money for Hawaii. At this point, living in San Francisco is like living with a woman you want to get away from but are too lazy to break things off with because you're comfortable and you don't want to be alone. But you're alone.

Look, I'm doing the right thing. Things are better than they were last month, the month before that, and the past few months before that. I just took a cush new job working 4:00 pm to midnight five days a week. I sit at a little desk at an upscale condominium complex, I play music, and I write. I'm basically getting paid to do what I love. I'm a writer, so I write. It's not glamorous, but everything is working out. What more could I want?

WHAT TO EXPECT AT YOUR FIRST TWELVE-STEP MEETING

Are you an addict of some kind? Yes? No? Maybe? Have you ever been to a twelve-step meeting? Are you curious? Maybe a friend or family member asked you to go to an AA meeting for support? If none of this applies to you, how did you get ahold of this book?

My first twelve-step meeting was an Al-Anon meeting. What is Al-Anon? Good question. Al-Anon is a worldwide fellowship that offers a program of recovery for families and friends of alcoholics. If you're related to an alcoholic or have a friend who is an addict and fear for their life and you just don't know what to do or where to go for help, Al-Anon might be the place for you. Al-Anon is a place for someone who is drowning in someone else's crazy shit. Al-Anon is where many people find out they're extremely codependent and need just as much help as the addict they've been trying to help. A good Al-Anon meeting will teach you the ABCs of codependency, denial, and how to love the addict you're trying to help from a distance. Many Al-Anon members eventually join other twelve-step programs such as CODA and ACA.

CODA stands for Codependents Anonymous. CODA is another solid twelve-step program for people who share a common desire to develop functional and healthy relationships. After spending some time in Al-Anon, many members realize that most, if not all, of their relationships are dysfunctional. Relationships with family, past lovers, platonic friendships, work relationships, and current marriage partners. If you have made it into a CODA meeting and can relate to what everyone is saying, you're definitely a codependent personality type and may have a long road ahead of you. I went to CODA meetings regularly for a couple of years, and it really helped me out. I found CODA meetings while going to AA meetings for some time, and I was just looking for something more. None of my relationships were going well, and I wasn't solving my problem with AA alone. CODA helped me see just how blind I was to all my poor relationship habits and my low self-esteem. I didn't think I deserved to be around quality people.

Eventually, my work in CODA led me to what I believe to be the most intense twelve-step program available: ACA, which stands for Adult Children of Alcoholics and Dysfunctional Families. ACA attracts the type of person who wants to belong to the Navy Seals of twelve-step groups. Working the twelve-steps of ACA is the hardest thing I have ever done in my life. If you have been to an ACA meeting already or are interested in attending an ACA meeting, you probably come from a very dysfunctional family—abuse, neglect, and mental health issues, whether your own or people in your family, who abused, neglected, and had mental health issues. If you have made it to ACA, you have made it to the very tippy top of the twelve-step mountain. Since my sobriety date of 11.26.01, I have experienced multiple forms of therapy, the medical industry and its doctors and medication, and six different twelve-step programs, and I'm convinced that ACA crushes them all.

I'm convinced that if we can find a way to learn that we all have something to give to the world, that we matter and deserve to love and be loved, we will no longer need drugs, alcohol, food, sex, and money the way we always seemed to need these things. Yes, money is an important tool because it allows us to have food, shelter, clothing, and education. But money is not God. My low self-esteem is the reason behind all my obsessive thinking. My lack of self-worth is behind all my cravings for booze, sex, food, and money. When I feel good about myself, all that other shit disappears. Today, when I feel the need to watch a little porn or eat a giant sandwich at two in the morning, I know something is up. Something is going on inside my mind. And this is where prayer and meditation come in. This is when I need God. I say this after many years of convincing myself that I don't need a higher power. All I need is myself. I'm smart. I'm strong. I can fix anything and everything that comes my way.

But if this were true, I'd be fine all the time. But I'm not fine all the time. I'm not always doing great. Shit happens in life. Family and friends die before they should. Jobs come and go. Lovers break up, money is owed to the tax man. Shit happens, people! Shit happens, and I can't always take it all on by myself. I need people, and I need my higher power to help me through sometimes. I have known this for many years, but it took many more years for me to accept this. Addiction of any kind will take many years to get a handle on. Addiction is a motherfucker, and it doesn't quit.

I'm not saying this to scare you. I'm telling you this so you have an edge. I'm giving you a cheat sheet on what to expect with your addiction or a loved one's addiction. I wish I knew this shit when I first got sober. I wish I knew at the age of twenty-two what addiction really was. I wish someone had told me that I was a complete codependent mess and what that meant as well. There are so many layers to being a drunk, a sex addict, or a food junkie. It's not about putting the drink down and you're sober, no. It's about the feelings you have now and why you have them. What happened when you were four years old? Why do you hate yourself today? Recovery is about digging deep and facing the people, places, and things that fucked you up. If you don't figure this shit out, the booze will come back. You will keep losing jobs, your family will most likely never talk to you again, and sadly, there's a good chance you will experience such lows in your head to the point that you will convince yourself that the only escape from all this is simply ending it. Yes, madness, prison, and death are all possibilities for any addict who refuses to face their fears. This happens to thousands of people every day.

I wrote this book because I'd like to help someone not go down that dark path. If I can help you convince yourself that you're worth a better life, then that's what this book is all about. I hope you decide to try a twelve-step meeting soon. It could save your life. These meetings sure have saved mine.

DO YOU REALLY WANT
TO GET SOBER?

If you want to get sober, there are only a few things you need to do. It's really not that hard. I'll even write a list of shit you need to do.

1. **Decide You're Done:** You have to decide that this is it. You're finally fucking done. You're done with the booze, the coke, the gambling, eating yourself to death, you name it. You have to be done.

2. **Find Meetings:** The next thing you need to do is google the city you live in and the twelve-step meeting you need to go to. If you live in Philadelphia and want to stop drinking for good, google "Philadelphia AA meetings." Or if you live in Tacoma, Washington, and want to stop gambling, just google "Tacoma Gamblers Anonymous meetings." Whatever it is that you're trying to quit, there's a meeting for it. Pretty easy so far, right?

3. Attend Your First Meeting: At your first twelve-step meeting, there will be a guy at the front of the meeting called a secretary. He's not the boss; he's just someone who helps keep that meeting organized. Eventually, he will ask if there are any newcomers at the meeting. You're a newcomer. Raise your hand, tell the room your first name and that you're an alcoholic or sex addict or whatever you are in that moment.

4. Speak Up: Toward the end of the meeting, you might be given the chance to speak for a couple of minutes. Just reintroduce yourself to the room. Tell the room you're trying to get sober and you need some help. Also, and this is important, tell the room that you need a sponsor and you'd like to start working the twelve steps as soon as possible. Most likely, someone with some sober time will approach you after the meeting and offer to be your sponsor. If this doesn't happen after your first meeting, just keep going to meetings and keep repeating to the room that you need a sponsor. You'll find someone in no time. A sponsor will be instrumental in helping you stay sober. I'll talk more about sponsors later.

5. Focus on Health: Once you have a sponsor and you're working the twelve steps, you're going to want to start looking into your overall health. Join a gym, learn how to eat right. If you're drinking energy drinks, eating fast food, and smoking cigarettes, you're going to want to stop that shit as soon as possible. That shit will kill you just as fast as whatever you used to do every day.

6. No Relationships for a Year: Don't hook up with people at your twelve-step meetings. This is suicide on so many levels. It doesn't matter if you're into men, women, or everything in between. No relationships. I wouldn't recommend casual sex either. No addict knows how to have casual sex. Remember, you're trying to stay sober, not hit it and quit it. Just focus on sobriety and your health for a solid year. Trust me.

7. Get a Commitment: Get a commitment at one of your regular meetings. Start making coffee before the meeting starts or become a greeter. Say hi to people. Offer to put chairs away. Fucking do something. If you're not sure how to get started, walk up to the meeting secretary and tell them you need to find a commitment as soon

as possible. This will definitely help you stay sober.

8. Help Others: Once you finish the twelve steps with your sponsor, try to get a sponsee as soon as you can. Help someone newer than you go through the twelve steps. If you can do all the things I just listed, you will most likely stay sober. Only you can fuck this up. It doesn't matter where you live or how much money you have (or don't have). It doesn't matter who your parents are, and it doesn't matter who you used to be. The past is the past. Now get to work. And good luck!

RONNIE'S BRILLIANT TAKE
ON STEPS EIGHT AND NINE

Last night, my sponsee and good buddy, Ronnie, stopped by my office while I was working, and we decided to do some more step work together. About four years ago, just before Covid hit, Ronnie and I tried working the steps together, but Ronnie wasn't ready. Ronnie is a couple of years older than me, but he acts like a teenager sometimes. I think Ronnie's eternal youth and immaturity are part of what I like about him. Ronnie is hilarious, and I love to laugh at inappropriate things as often as I can. So, when Ronnie and I get together, we like to get loud, rude, and crude. Even sober, I can see us getting kicked out of a restaurant or a museum together for disturbing the peace.

I ran into Ronnie about two weeks ago at the Dry Dock, and I was so happy to see him again. The last time I saw him, he was going through one of his manic highs, but this time around, Ronnie seemed to have his shit together. We talked before and after the AA meeting. It was so good to see Ronnie in a good place.

The world is more fun to live in when Ronnie is in a healthy place. We exchanged numbers again that night, and by the time I got home, Ronnie texted me and asked if I would sponsor him. With hesitation, I said yes. Never turn another man down if he wants to try getting sober. We met the next day at the Dry Dock and got right into step one. We read through the 12x12 book, and we decided to cruise through steps One, Two, and Three. We talked about what we read and hit a meeting, then we met the next day at the Dry Dock.

I had Ronnie write down everyone he had a resentment against. When Ronnie was ready, he went through everyone on his list, talked about each situation in depth, and after a couple of hours, we were ready to move on to step six. Working the steps with Ronnie so far has been a blast. When someone is ready to change their life, the steps and everything else can move fast. It doesn't have to take eighteen months to work the twelve-steps of Alcoholics Anonymous. Back in the old days, when AA first got started, guys were going through the steps in a few days and then helping other guys get sober. Today, people will sit on a step for months at a time. Why? What's the fuckin' point? Today, I think a lot of people just need attention. So many people walk into meetings because nobody else will talk to them. They get sober for a few months or a year, get their families and jobs back, and then quit AA. Almost 100% of the time, those same people relapse, and they're back at square one—or worse.

Last night, Ronnie and I got together, read through steps six and seven, talked about them, and then moved on to step eight. Luckily, Ronnie had already written down a bunch of names of people and places he felt he needed to make amends to. Ronnie's list is so great I felt I should share it with you.

***

Ronnie: "Dear Lyft, I'm sorry for driving drunk and high at times while picking up customers. I'm also sorry for flirting with male customers. It was illegal, reckless, and careless. I'm both embarrassed and grateful that I hurt no one. To make up for this, I'm going to do twelve hours of charity work.

"Dear Uber, I drove drunk and high while on the platform. I also picked up on men while on the platform. My behavior was gross and inappropriate. As amends, I will do twelve hours of charity.

"Dear Instacart and everyone concerned, I'm sorry for stealing from your customers, especially during Covid. I'm sorry for eating people's groceries, and I'm sorry for using the company card for myself. It was dishonest, selfish, and reckless. I'd like to make amends through twelve hours of charity work.

"Sincerely, Ronnie."

Mark: "What else do you got?"

Ronnie: "Dear Whole Foods, I stole from you. I lied to get hired. I never charged any of the cute white men for their groceries. Like, ever."

Mark: (Laughing) "Really? You never charged men you were attracted to for their groceries?"

Ronnie: (Laughing) "No! Like never!" I just couldn't. They were just too cute. After a while, the word got out, and all these white men would be in my line and refuse the help of other employees. I don't know, it just didn't make sense to me that hot guys should pay for their groceries. I also stole thousands of dollars' worth of food from Whole Foods."

Mark: "Seriously?"

We both laughed.

Ronnie: "This is over a twenty-year period, you know. And I know this is wrong, and I'd like to make amends and promise to not live like that anymore. I also am going to do twelve hours of volunteer work to make amends."

Mark: "Okay."

Ronnie: "Dear Macy's, I stole clothes and fragrances from you. When you hired me, I flaked and didn't show up for my shifts. I got fired. I would get all these jobs when I was young. When I was younger, I was like this little golden child. I would just put on some slacks and a black shirt, spray on some cologne, and I would get hired, like that. But I would always flake on everybody. I did the same thing when I was in school. I got shitty grades, but everybody loved me, so nobody ever did anything. I was a fuck-up, Mark."

Ronnie and I couldn't help ourselves from laughing about Ronnie's self-deprecation. A major part of

Ronnie's addiction and self-destruction seemed to be his compulsive need to steal and give up on himself, whether it be his education or work life. I can relate to this. I was guilty of fucking off at school and work when I was younger.

Ronnie: "Dear Safeway."

Mark: (Laughing) "Dear Safeway?"

Ronnie: "Dear Safeway, you hired me a few times over the years, and I never showed up for work. I also stole food when I shopped there. I would hide steaks in my backpack and just pay for the cheaper items. I didn't charge some customers for their groceries, and I stole twenty dollars in cash one evening. I know this is not acceptable, and I never want to steal again. To make amends, I will commit to twelve hours of charity work.

"Dear Marin Brewing Company?"

Mark: "Marin Brewing Company?"

Ronnie: "Marin Brewing Company, I was a waiter there when I was cute and twenty-five. So, dear Marin Brewing Company, I showed up to work on drugs, I was a flake, and a shitty employee. As amends, twelve more hours of charity volunteer work.

"Dear Target."

We both started cracking up again. Ronnie has worked for half of the companies in San Francisco and has fucked them all over one way or another.

Ronnie: "Dear Target, I have stolen so much from you guys. It's appalling and awful. To make amends, I will commit to yet another twelve hours of volunteer work.

"Dear Trader Joe's, I got hired twice and just quit because I was spoiled. It was sad and crazy behavior. I have also stolen a lot from you in the past. As amends—"

Mark: "Twelve hours."

Ronnie: "Twelve more hours."

Mark: "Any more?"

Ronnie: (Laughing) "Oh, hell yeah, brother. Sephora, Mac, Nordstrom, Sears, Starbucks, Peet's, Wells Fargo, Bank of America, Chase."

Mark: "These are all places you have worked?"

Ronnie: "Some, but I have stolen from all of them, so I owe like 5,000 hours of community service or something like that. Like I said, everywhere I applied to, they would just hire me. I mean, I went to the French American School, I speak a little Spanish, and I just can't stop smiling, so people wanted me back then. But now, when I try getting a job, people just look at me and think, *Who the fuck is this fool? What's his fucking story?* Nobody is hiring me now."

Mark: "Yeah, I get that."

Ronnie: "Oh! Oh, this one is important because I wanna pay this back. I owe thirty-five dollars and I've owed it for years, but it's to this little store over on Church and Market. Because I went in one day, this guy was working in this cute little store with groceries right next to the Mexican place, and I just went in one day and introduced myself. So I asked the guy in the cute little grocery store if I could grab 35 bucks worth of groceries, and he let me."

Mark: "Oh, I see, you just never paid the guy back and you feel bad."

Ronnie: "Yeah, I feel hella shitty about it. But I also want to talk about Chinese restaurants. I definitely have that disorder where I have Chinese Restaurant Syndrome, where I was hooked on fucking Chinese food."

Mark: "Totally! I definitely had that for a couple of years."

Ronnie: "For years, I would scam Chinese food restaurants by talking to them a lot and distracting them, and they would forget to charge me."

Mark and Ronnie laughing up a storm.

Ronnie: "So I owe like fifty Chinese food restaurants a bunch of cash, so I should just take on a couple hundred more hours of volunteer work right there. I just want to acknowledge all this. I know I was a scumbag for years."

Mark: "Got it."

Ronnie: "Harrison, my ex-fiancé—I was with him for four years."

Mark: "How long ago was this? How old were you?"

Ronnie: "We were together from 2003 to 2007. I was twenty-six to thirty. So, although we were a couple and it was my money as well, and I was bringing in a ton of money back then, I did embezzle money from Harrison for months. I got the idea from watching an episode of *Law & Order SVU*. I remember Mariska Hargitay saying something about the fact that most women who get out of abusive marriages always have a plan. They usually put small amounts of money away for six months and then finally disappear.

"Harrison never physically abused me, of course. That was never even going to fuckin' happen, I would fuck somebody up. But mentally, he was a lot smarter than me, so he was super mentally abusive, right, and he was a drunk, a bad drunk."

Mark: "Oh, really?"

Ronnie: "Really. But he was a lovely man, but…"

Mark: "He was an alcoholic."

Ronnie: "Bad, I mean really bad back then, right. But I don't think he is anymore. But my friends stalk all my exes on social media, so I have to hear from Lisa and Holly everything that is going on with these men. But before I left Harrison, I put away money for six months. I bought a car, got an apartment in Santa Rosa, grabbed my cat, and I was gone, bro.

"Oh, and this Jewish family, the Dunworths, they have a really famous artist in the family, and they're like super-rich philanthropists. Well, they're really old now, but I was really good friends with their daughter. I told them that I was engaged to be married, and at that point, gay marriage was legal. But it became illegal right before our wedding date. This wasn't even a joke. And I was young and attractive, and at the time, my family and my cousins were all ready to go to the big wedding reception party that we had planned.

Harrison would spare no expense. He made so much money, and life was so good in the early 2000s for us."

Mark: "And how old was Harrison?"

Ronnie: "Ten years older than me."

Mark: "Okay."

Ronnie: "So, Harrison, and… what, Brian? Brian was the first boyfriend I ever lived with. We were in Mill Valley together for two years. And, I don't know, honestly, there's a balance between Brian and me because he owes my family money. He owes my cousin John money. My cousin John is a cop, and I owe him like $6,000."

Mark: "You owe your cousin John money?"

Ronnie: "Yeah, and it's weird because my whole family—all the women, like my mom, his mom, my sisters, my girl cousins—they're like, 'Only you could have borrowed money from John, let alone $6,000.' I was going to pay him right back. I forget what happened, but it just kind of fell to the side. My grandmother even said that the only reason John gave me money is because he knows it's as good as gold. And I will pay him back.

"Anyways, I knew Angella, this realtor, and she told me the house I was living in in Mill Valley was for sale, so I took all the furniture in the house and used it to furnish my next place. But I did find a way to pay her back because I found a way for her to sell one of my grandparents' properties, so Angella let me slide."

Mark: "Okay, so these are people that are on your list that you stole from and want to pay back?"

Ronnie: "Right! Well, a couple of them. Oh, and there's also Lucky's, Walgreens, Rite Aid—"

Mark: "Oh, so did you work for these places, or did you steal from them?"

Ronnie: "Yeah, I worked at Lucky's for one night, I stole from Walgreens all the time, Rite Aid I ripped off blind for years. Sometimes I feel these places went out of business because of me, you know. I stole from CVS on occasion, but not that much.

"Um, I grabbed a cop's dick. One time, I was getting arrested—the one time I was getting arrested, I should say. I was in some store, and these two fine-ass cops were arresting me. I was like thirty-three, and I was out of my mind on meth, but it turns out my uncle was there, but I didn't say anything because I was kind of interested in the process of getting arrested. Like, what's going to happen? I was kind of into it. So, they put me in their car, and when I get out of the car, I grabbed his dick, and he was so embarrassed and so shocked, and his partner was like, 'What just happened?' The cop whose dick I grabbed said that I tried to grab his gun. I honestly didn't even care. So, they put me in the tank or whatever it's called. Basically, the cops found out that my uncle was a sergeant. Oh, because I called my mom. My mom must have called my uncle. The cops came in yelling at me and told me I should have let them know who my uncle was. They let me know that I wasn't going to jail, but because I was high as fuck and out of my mind, they were going to 5150 me. But I was so out of it, and I was kind of feeling myself because I was swimming and running every day. I was trying to get in shape because this girlfriend of mine was getting married, and I was going to go to this big firefighter wedding, and there are so many hot firemen in San Francisco, and the afterparty was going to be on a yacht.

"So, I'm hella feeling myself, and I'm all arrested and crazy, and there's nothing but cute white cops where I'm being held, so I just started jacking off, right."

Mark: "Wait, where were you? You were jacking off next to police officers?"

Ronnie: "18th and Bryant, the area where you're arrested. So, I'm flying high, and I'm jacking off, I'm such a fucking perv, Mark."

Mark: "Jesus, Ronnie!"

Ronnie: "I'm jacking off and talking dirty to myself, and just before I'm about to fucking nut, this fucking old Chinese lady comes pushing this shitty cart with peanut butter and jelly sandwiches, and she's looking right at me, and I'm coming right as this little old lady is looking at me. I was fucking mortified, and I knew right there that God was paying me back for my bullshit that night."

Mark: "What... the... hell... Ronnie?"

Ronnie: "Yeah, and my uncle and I have always fucked with each other, and as soon as my uncle heard about my jack-off story, he called me and started calling me all these Greek tragedies, and the whole thing is just so fucked up. Rather than having to go to jail or pay fines, I always found a way to get out of trouble, and the worst thing that would ever happen is that my uncle would bring up my stories to the whole family at Thanksgiving or some big family get-together.

"It's been a long road, dude."

Mark: "I guess so."

Ronnie: "Yeah. Um, my cousin Tessy and her boyfriend, my mom, 24 Hour Fitness, YMCA towels, Hulu."

Mark: "YMCA towels?"

Ronnie: "Oh hell yeah, man, I have like fifty YMCA towels now. I do owe my mom a tiny bit of money. And it doesn't matter how many gifts I buy my mom, if I owe her $5, she wants that $5 back. She's just a fucking lesbian like that, you know. Lesbians are super stingy with their money. I do owe a small amount in taxes.

"I tempted, propositioned, and paid Keaton for sex, and I feel bad about that because even though we're both consenting adults, I feel like part of the reason he is unhappy is because of the way things went down. Keaton's girlfriend found out about Keaton and me. I used to send messages to Keaton's girlfriend through social media, taunting her and telling her about all the things Keaton and I had done together.

"I also owe a barber $60, my high school I flaked on, medical and dental appointments I flaked on and never paid for. I gossip all the time, sex and love addiction. I need Debtors Anonymous, overeating, and I yell at people.

"Look, Mark, I'm a very honest person."

Mark: "Who lies a lot, right?"

Ronnie: "Pretty much. But not as much now. I'm forty-seven, and I just don't care what people think as much. But in my younger years and up 'til my early forties, yeah, I was lying a lot, for sure. Look, I'm not saying that I'm off the hook. I'm just saying that when you're matriculating in a society and you're hiding something, like being a homosexual, and that goes on into your later teens, it becomes a part of your personality."

Mark: "Sure, I think I know what you mean."

Ronnie: "And you use fake names when you hook up with guys, you're afraid they're going to find out where you live. You're worried that your family's going to find out, and so you use aliases. You're just lying all the time in order to stay safe.

"When I say these things, I hope that younger gay kids don't have to live the kind of lie I had to live or other older gay people had to live. When I see these younger gay kids wearing rainbow shirts at school and going to all the LGBTQ marches and events, I hope they have it better than I did when I was thirteen years old. If they do, I like to feel like my generation helped make things better for the younger gay kids, but I never forget that my generation paid dearly while growing up gay back in the day. A lot of us are fucked up. A lot of us are junkies, just because a lot of our families couldn't get their heads out of their asses and just let us be who we are without telling us God is going to kill us."

Mark: "Yeah, that's so heavy, Ronnie."

Ronnie: "Fuck yeah, it is. Like I remember when I was fifteen and I was hanging out on 25th Street at Judy Davis's house, and she was with Chet Helms, like that was her man, you know. They weren't married, but he was Bill Graham's best friend, and they discovered Janis Joplin. I was hanging out with Dana Crumb. I remember I was like fifteen, and Judy was trying to quit smoking."

Mark: "Crumb the cartoonist? Robert Crumb?"

Ronnie: "Yes, yes! And Hayden and Tessa were together, and my cousin married into this rock-and-roll family. Hayden, the one who committed suicide. She married into this major rock-and-roll family. Hayden and this family put on all these rock-and-roll shows in the city. And so this one night, I had cigarettes, and I would sneak Judy cigarettes, and we would hang out in the backyard. I remember Dana Crumb and Judy would show me pictures of Judy when she was a kid in Acapulco with her rich dad and pictures of them in Southern California. Judy and Dana would explain to me what revolutionists were. Back in the '40s, a lot of white girls who were born into money would end up going to college in the '60s, and they would be the first to learn that not everyone in the world has everything like they did. Today, through social media, everybody knows that the world isn't fair, but back then, only a small minority of people, mostly young white women, knew this.

"So in the '60s, there was all this campus unrest that we read about today. Haight-Ashbury, the movement happened. And then Obama made gay marriage legal, like federally legal. It's a big fucking deal, man. But the downside of all this is that since gay marriage is legal, I don't know if everyone was mature enough to handle it. A lot of gay couples with kids don't take responsibility for their kids, and the kids grow up to be fucked up like me. Both my parents are gay, and their partners later in life didn't want anything to do with me. I think if you're with somebody, if you're fucking somebody with kids, that kid is now yours, and you have to step up. You have to set a positive example for them. You don't just get to be a fuck-up lying around the house, you know what I mean? That's gross, man. It's unacceptable, and that's what I had to deal with growing up. You know, like my father's partner and my mother's partner both being jealous of me. The whole thing was hideous. It was fucking bizarre. But whatever, right? It is what it is, and we have to move on or go nuts or drink ourselves to death, right?"

Mark: "I hear you, Ronnie. Do you feel better?"

Ronnie: "Fuck yeah, man! That was intense! We gotta do this kind of shit more often."

Mark: "Cool, let's take a break."

CLOSE CALL

A couple of days ago, I got a text from my sponsee, Ronnie.

Ronnie: "Hey bro. I just wanted to let you know that I really appreciate you working the steps with me. I'd like to keep checking in with you on occasion, but I'm not going to go to meetings anymore. I just don't get anything from the meetings. I plan on staying sober, but I have so much stuff going on in my own life right now. All my best girlfriends are going through so much shit, and I have been trying to be there for them, but I don't have anything left to give. Thanks again for everything."

If you have been sober a while and have sponsored people over the years, maybe you have heard this before. Or maybe you have sent a past sponsor a text just like this. Ninety-two percent of the time, what follows a text or conversation like this is a relapse. Trust me, somebody is relapsing after that. Rather than getting all riled up and butthurt over this, I decided to give it twenty-four hours. I have learned that it is not a smart idea to chase a sponsee once they tell you they don't want to work the AA program anymore. I have chased a couple of sponsees in the past, and it just makes things worse. The next day, I texted Ronnie.

Mark: "Ronnie, I just want to say that I'm really enjoying working with you. You're a blast to spend time with. I also want to say that I don't recommend leaving the program and trying to stay sober on your own. I tried this once, and it was a fucked-up experience. Can you say depression? You have already been sober for eight months, and we just finished the twelve steps together. You're in a really good spot right now. I recommend you just pick one meeting you really like and start with that. If you like the Castro meetings, please keep going. If you need to find another sponsor, please try that. I just hope you don't give up on AA. There are a lot of great people in the program. I know it can be a pain in the ass to find a group of friends you actually like, but I know they're out there. Let's talk soon."

Later that same day, Ronnie called me.

Ronnie: "What's up, BIIIAAATCH?!?"

Mark: "Ronnie! You're alive!"

Ronnie: "Hell yeah, brutha! Hey, I just wanted to apologize for my shitty text. You're right, I can't quit AA. I can't do this shit on my own."

Mark: "It's cool, man."

Ronnie: "I wanna keep working with you, bro. My friend Mandy is in the middle of a divorce, and my friend Dina just moved back to SF, and her entire family hates the guy she brought back from Hawaii. He's using her for her family's money, and it's just a lot, bro."

Mark: "Okay, I get it, but I want to ask you something, and please, don't feel like I'm judging, because I'm not."

Ronnie: "Cool, okay."

Mark: "So, all of this shit going on with your friends. What does it have to do with you and your sobriety? I don't understand, and I wanted to see if you could walk me through why you're so affected by your friends' lives to the point that you're exhausted and willing to give up your AA program and put your sobriety at risk."

Ronnie: "Fuck, dude, I know it's crazy. I just want to help my friends."

Mark: "Okay, I get that, man, but how is giving up on your health going to help anyone? Do you see what I'm saying?"

Ronnie: "Oh, totally, man. I totally get it. What do you think I should do?"

Mark: "Well, this is a tricky question. I don't want to tell you what to do, but I will tell you what I would do today if I were in your position. I would continue to go to AA meetings, and I would set boundaries with my friends that I feel are taking too much of my energy away from me. Why can't you listen to your friends but not take it personally? You act like your friends' problems are your problems, but they aren't. You're not married. You don't have children. You're a single man, you live alone, you don't really have any major responsibilities right now. Am I right?"

Ronnie: "Yeah, fuck yeah, you're right!"

Mark: "I think you might just be bored. Maybe you're lacking purpose, and this is why you get so involved in your friends' drama. Their shit might just be keeping you busy."

Ronnie: "Fuck, man, that's fucked up."

Mark: "It's just a possibility."

Ronnie: "What should I do?"

Mark: "I'd find shit to do. In your case, I'd hit a meeting every day. I'd go to the gym. I'd write books, meet friends for coffee. This is shit that I personally do. I'm not saying you should write books or go to the gym, but you're always talking about losing weight. That seems to be a big thing with you. I would make your health one of the top three things you focus on. Sobriety, exercise, and whatever your third thing is. Focus on three things, and that will eat up a lot of your day. If you want to work, look for a job. Work could be your third thing."

Ronnie: "You make it sound so easy."

Mark: "Changing your whole life is scary. I get that. We're junkies. We don't like change. But you have the luxury of time right now. You don't really have to be a part of the rat race, which is a gift. You can just focus on yourself right now. Most people can't do that. Most addicts that are trying to get their life together and stay sober also have to work shitty jobs that they don't want, which take up time and energy. Be grateful that you don't have to do this. It's a beautiful thing, Ronnie. Just be blessed."

Ronnie: "Fuck, man! This is great!"

Mark: "Write down what you have to do today and just think about these things. That's what I have to do. Even if it's only three or four things, just write it down. If you start thinking too much and getting bitchy and cranky, just look at your list."

Ronnie: "Does that actually work?"

Mark: "I swear to God it works. I have been doing this for a couple of months, and it has really helped free up some space in my head."

Ronnie: "Thanks for taking my call. I hope we can keep working together. I'm learning so much, and I want to do this. I was just having a fucked-up day. I want to do this, Mark."

Mark: "Cool! Let's keep going then. Next time you have a shitty day, just call or text. You don't have to quit everything in your life and disappear. We all have shit days. It's totally cool. If you need to talk, feel free to call me later. I'll be around."

Ronnie: "Awesome! I'll call you later. See ya."

Click.

THE LITTLE BOAT

If you were to ask me today what it's like to be an addict or to come from a dysfunctional family of addicts, I think I have the perfect story for you. It's a simple story and I think it will get my point across. Let me try.

There was once a family: a mother, a father, two sons, and one daughter. The oldest boy was fourteen. The middle child, the daughter, was twelve. And the youngest, the golden boy, was six years old. The mother was a stay-at-home mom who volunteered two weekends a month at the local library. The father was a successful real estate agent.

One day, the father was a little late coming home from work, but with good reason. He brought home a small motorboat with just enough room for five people. The family lived just two miles from a beautiful lake that allowed boats like the one. The whole family came running out to see their new boat. The children were bursting with excitement. The mother, a little more cautious and almost hesitant, put on her best face. This family had hit a bit of a rough patch with money over the past few months. The father hadn't been selling many houses, and that made the mother nervous. She had grown up very poor, and the first thing she did when she married was make the father promise her that she would never have to be poor again. The father made this promise.

As the children danced around the boat with excitement, the mother quietly asked the father if they could afford this new boat.

"Of course we can, dear. Everything will be just fine. You'll see," said the father.

The mother remained skeptical, but again, she put her happy face back on.

The father made an announcement to the family. "Everybody, this weekend we will take out the boat and have a great time!"

The children cheered. The mother was happy that her children were so excited. Their joy created a sense of calm for her.

A few days later, the family took their new boat for its first afternoon joyride. On the way to the lake, they sang along to The Beatles' *Abbey Road*, which heightened the joyous occasion.

Soon after getting into the boat, everyone put on their bright orange life jackets.

"We can never be too careful," said the father.

The mother took sandwiches and juice out of the family cooler. The father started the boat, and the family was on their way. After ten minutes or so, the middle child, the daughter, felt cold water on her feet. She looked down and saw a small hole with water coming up onto the boat.

"Mom! Dad! Look, there's a hole in the boat. Water is everywhere!"

"Oh, no!" said the mother.

"Oh, everything will be just fine. There's nothing to worry about. Just relax, everybody," said the father.

"But honey, we have to go back to shore. The boat will fill up with water and we will sink," said the mother.

The mother, both sons, and the daughter all looked at each other with confusion. They had never seen the father act like this before.

"Come on, Dad, let's go back. If we don't go back soon, we'll have to swim back," said the oldest son.

"Nonsense! We aren't going to let a little water spoil our fun," said the father.

"But, Dad, it's not just a little bit of water. There's a lot of water in the boat, and it's not going to stop until we get back to land and have this problem looked at," said the oldest son.

"Oh, so now you know everything about boats?" said the father. "We aren't going back, so just get comfortable and have fun. Nothing bad will happen."

More and more water made its way into the boat. Soon the water reached the family's ankles. The father ignored the fact that more water was entering the boat. He just went faster and faster.

"See, guys, isn't this fun? I can't believe you wanted to go back. I told you everything was going to be fine," said the father.

The family quietly sat on the boat, praying that the father would eventually bring the boat back to land. Soon the water reached the family's calves. Water splashed everywhere. The boat's engine began to make a strange noise. Soon smoke spewed from the engine.

"Dad! Look! The engine is smoking," said the daughter.

"Oh, daughter, you worry too much. I'll look at it when we get back home. Everything's fine!"

"What's wrong with you? Go back now! You're scaring the children, and you're scaring me," said the mother.

"I'll go back when I'm good and ready! Just a few more minutes," said the father.

The oldest son jumped off the boat and started swimming for land. A few seconds later, the youngest son followed. At the same time, the boat's engine caught fire, and there was a small explosion.

The mother and daughter screamed, "Help! Help us!"

"Calm down! Stop screaming," said the father.

The oldest son finally made it back to shore. As soon as he looked back at the boat and his family, he saw that the flames from the engine were getting bigger. He could hear his father yelling at his mother and younger sister. Soon, two fire trucks arrived. The firemen put out the boat fire and helped tow the boat back to shore. The father, mother, and daughter were all safe and sound. The father talked with the firemen.

The mother looked around and asked, "Where's your little brother?"

"I thought he was with you," said the older brother.

"No, he jumped off the boat after you," said the mother.

The mother, older brother, and sister immediately started looking for the younger brother. Soon the father and the firemen joined in the search. Quite some time passed, and the sun began to go down.

Out of nowhere, the younger sister screamed. "Oh no! I found him! Come quick!"

A fireman rushed over to the little sister, where he found the younger brother's lifeless body in the water just inches from land. The younger brother had drowned, and there was nothing anyone could do.

More and more people gathered around to see what was happening. The entire family, in shock, stared at the younger brother.

"What have I done?" said the father.

The mother took one last hard look at the father. Her eyes clearly told him that nothing would ever be the same. Nothing could ever be the same again.

We can only imagine what happened to this family. Who knows what the future holds for the father, mother, the oldest son, and daughter? We can only pray for each and every one of them. This once-happy group of people was immediately destroyed by one mistake. One act, one unfortunate occasion. Who will heal from this? All of them? None of them?

Again, we can only pray for them. We can hope that forgiveness and love will one day shine on these people. We can only pray.

RONNIE'S EXPERIENCE, STRENGTH, AND HOPE

I've been enjoying my time working with Ronnie in AA. I'm not going to lie, though. There has been some drama. Ronnie can be a bit extra at times, but I can relate to his mood swings and emotional outbursts. Yes, Ronnie has changed his phone number twice in the past eight days, and he told me a couple of times that he doesn't think AA works for him. But when we hang out and actually do the work, Ronnie is a pleasure to be around. Ronnie is a big personality. He's loud, brash, sharp, and hilarious. All of this makes the bumps in the road with Ronnie worth it.

I recently asked Ronnie if I could record his story of addiction and road to recovery and put it in my book. Well, he obviously said yes. I know I'm probably breaking some of AA's traditions by writing this book, but this is art. I'm an artist, and I make art. With that said, here's Ronnie.

***

Ronnie: "Hi, I'm Ronnie, and I'm an alcoholic. I'm forty-seven, born and raised in San Francisco,

California, and, well, my drug of choice was definitely, and unfortunately still is, crystal meth. I'm definitely a blackout drinker. So, what was it like? It was like… when you walked into the house I grew up in, there was this picture. A portrait, a big portrait of me and two of my first cousins. I was standing in the middle. It was 1979. I'm wearing a little white suit. My cousin Tessa is to the right of me in a little girl's suit with a white skirt and a scarf around her neck, and my cousin John is to the left of me in a dark blue suit. We're like four or five years old, and I'm two. We're at the Japanese Tea Gardens on our way to a first-class flight to Honolulu to celebrate my grandparents' thirty-fifth wedding anniversary, where they had condos.

"This portrait, when you walk into the house I grew up in, captured this moment in time where my hair was gold, and I was this pretty little baby. And I'm telling you, I was beautiful. People would always walk in and be so excited to see me. So, what it was like was, there was this innate sense of beauty in me and lots of love. I had eight grandparents. All of my dad's parents were alive, and all my mom's parents were alive. They were all just there, and they all loved me. The way I saw it, there was all this love, and I never thought about what I didn't have. I didn't really get on that trip until I started hanging out with other people. And you know, a lot of people become sheep in a way. They start complaining about not having a lot of things. That was a learned thing that I didn't start doing till I was in middle school. I wasn't around the "I don't haves" and the "poor me" people in the beginning. Early on, everyone was just different. Everybody I grew up with in San Francisco was different. All I know is that it was bliss when I was a kid. Ignorance is bliss when you're young.

"But there was always this problem, though, like, on the outside. I grew up thinking that everything was a problem on the outside. Because of the way my family raised me. All my grandparents sent all the same messages. Eight grandparents, four different families. They all believed that if it looks okay, then it's okay. And I don't know what happened, but God decided I was going to be the fat one. I wasn't just born pretty; I was also born fat. So everybody around me just wanted to get me thin. And then I got tall, so everybody wanted to get me buff, and my uncles always wanted me to play sports, so I tried playing sports. My aunts got me on drugs when I was young. And of course, the drugs worked until they didn't work, right? And I thought if I looked a certain way, everything would be okay.

"Five years, ten years, twenty years, and how old am I now? I'm forty-seven. So we're talking about thirty-three years ago when I was fourteen, I was on a mission. I just wanted to be slim and attractive. I went to this high school, School of the Arts, and a lot of people, when they were eighteen, were moving to LA to be discovered. I never went. I never thought I was thin enough or pretty enough. And I remember telling my mom one time in high school that I wanted to be an actor, and she told me that the world needs ugly actors too. At the time, I thought that was the meanest thing in the world to say, and years later, I heard Meryl Streep say the exact same thing. Meryl's mom said the exact same thing to her. I knew then that's just what parents say to their kids.

"So why am I telling you this? I guess because life isn't perfect. People aren't perfect. Even though I had eight grandparents, a mom, and all my aunts, there was nobody to take care of me when I was a little kid. I'm not saying that's what fucked me up, but it didn't help. My grandparents were too busy to take care of my mom, but she had housekeepers. But there were no housekeepers to take care of me when I was a kid, and I was raised in my mom's house. In a three-story, nine-bedroom cliff house in San Francisco, Mount Davidson. It was chaos! It was fucking chaos. I had aunts coming back and forth. They would lose houses or apartments. They would break up with their husbands or get into fights with their boyfriends, come home with another kid, and then get a bunch of money from my grandparents or start getting drugs from my mom. It was just a mess. It was a fucked-up scene. And I didn't know this was fucked up. It's just what it was, I guess.

"But I was kind of smart when I was a kid. I was always in honors classes, and I was also friends with the smart white girls and Chinese girls that were going places in life. I don't know what happened to me, though. I just know that drugs and alcohol took a toll on me. I know that the first time I got drunk, I was twelve, and I blacked out. I started using narcotics when I was fourteen. I stopped using narcotics when I turned thirty-three. I realized I was a blackout drunk. I kept blacking out for like a year before I found the rooms. Because I realized you can be really drunk and really awake if you're on coke or speed. But if you're not, and you're just drinking, you just become a big fucking lump.

"So I came to the rooms, and I fucking hated it. I remember the first time I went to a meeting in the Castro, I walked in, and I didn't want to be there. It was at the Most Holy Redeemer Church, and there were all these gay guys there, and they were all being totally rude. They wouldn't talk to me, right? I swear to God. And I raised my hand and yelled out, 'I'm not gonna fucking do this! I don't want to be around any of you, but I have to be here to save my life! You guys are all pulling your little pretty shit, and half of you aren't even that pretty, and I'm not going to put up with any of your little fucking games!' I fucking reamed them, dude. 'I'm sick of this fucking bullshit, you guys! I had to deal with it when I was high, and I'm not going to deal with it while I try to get sober.'

"And, at the end of that meeting, all these gay guys gave me their numbers. It's not even what I was going for, but the magic I found with all these people I just screamed at. These people just seemed to have their shit together. I started to get invited to these sober parties, and I went on a sober trip to Yosemite, and some of them gave me a job at this really elite gym, and they paid me under the table. They were all hooking me up. I got a sponsor who was a doctor, and his sponsor was a Buddhist monk. I watched this magic of a sponsor who was an anesthesiologist, and he had no interest in religion, but he had no choice because of who his sponsor was. So, there was this weird magic that happened, but I wasn't ready to work the steps. I wasn't ready to be honest and thorough. So I stayed around the rooms, and I worked with him for a while, and I got the magic, and I realized where I needed to be, and I needed to be sober. Five years went by, but they weren't the greatest, but thank God for that time.

"Looking back, I'm so grateful because when I relapsed at forty, after being sober from thirty-four to forty, I started hanging out with the same people I'd been hanging out with years before. These people were so desolate. They were broke, always in trouble, and singing the same song—blaming the fucking police, their parents, and everyone else but themselves. I was lightyears beyond that because I'd spent the last five years plus sober and hanging out with sober, productive people. Not on purpose. Not as a fuck you to anybody. It's just the way it happened for me, and what a fucking blessing. I was hooked, and I knew sobriety and AA were the answer for me. And even knowing this, I had lots of relapses, unfortunately.

"I got together another two and a half years, and then I had a horrible fifteen-month relapse up until this last August of 2023. I started smoking speed again, and life got really too easy for me. I didn't have to pay rent, I had a good income rolling in, I was getting free drugs, and I was doing whatever I wanted. And I came to one day and I was like, 'No! This is not okay!' I was looking at an example of a man who was seventeen years older than me, and although he's a lovely person, and I don't want to say anything bad about him, he's fucked up. He's really sick, you know. He's always on drugs, and I don't want to be that. I don't want that. I want more, right?

"The cool thing about sobriety is when you're sober, you don't age fast. I knew that because I was raised by one of my grandmas, who was a high-class woman and an athlete. She was a golfer. She would always laugh at people who would complain about feeling old. She would always tell me that was low-class mentality. People like that don't age well. She would always remind me back when she was in her sixties that she was thriving, and she was. She always looked amazing! She was also always sober, and she was against smoking cigarettes. My grandfather was an alcoholic but wasn't.

"The beauty of sobriety is it gives you this life. It gives you these extra amazing years to do something amazing with your life. You get to be productive and help people. And you know, I still slip up and might fuck someone over by snapping at them, but on the flip side, five or six people might tell me that I really helped them. I'm starting to see this more and more as time goes by, which is nice. It's nice being a helpful person, you know.

"What it's like today, I think I want to go on record saying, whatever the higher power is or whatever your higher power is, it does put you on some kind of payroll. There's nobody that I've ever seen in the fucking rooms not guaranteed to be taken care of in one way or another. Everyone that wants to get sober and stay sober and work the program in the rooms will always be just fine. Everything will work out. All those things we worry about and lose sleep over won't happen if we just stay sober and in the room. God takes care of you. If you're willing to believe, God will take care of you. Everything that the ninth step promises talk about will come true for you. Every time I come back to the rooms, the ninth step promises always come back to me. But every time I leave the rooms and relapse, the promises also leave me.

"I think if you're thinking about getting sober and making a change in your life, all I can say is, just try. Just go to a meeting, walk through the day, and do everything that is suggested. For me, usually, things go my way when I stay sober and stay around people that are sober. I personally don't know how to deal with life when things fall out of place or alignment. I get overwhelmed and I fall apart. But when I stay close to my sponsor and the program, they help me keep my shit together. I don't want to go back to my old ways. So, I guess I'm still growing up in the rooms. It's weird. I've done weird shit in the rooms. I'm embarrassed to say I've asked guys to be my sponsor maybe because I just had dad issues or crushes. There are all these things that rear their ugly head in sobriety for me. There's lots of shit going on, but there are a lot of beautiful things going on as well. I've noticed if I keep trudging along, all the weirdness that is going on seems to iron itself out. And the cool thing is that in the room, there are a handful of solid people that haven't given up on me, and that's why I'm here. I love those people, and I trust them.

"I could go on and on about all this, but I think I should stop here. I'll end with this: I'm so grateful to be sober today, and if you want to be sober, you can, and I hope you choose to get help like I did. God Bless!"

THE ESCAPE ARTIST

What is this all about? All the drugs and acting out. Losing jobs, pissing people off, girlfriends and boyfriends breaking up with us. Why do we need to put all this nasty shit into our bodies? The alcohol, the drugs, the gambling, all the creepy sex. Why do we addicts do all this shit to ourselves and everyone around us? What the fuck is it all for?

So many people have theories about why we do this shit. Our doctors call it mental illness. Our fathers might say we have no self-control, and our mothers might think if we could just find the right partner, we could turn everything around. Everybody wants what's best for us, but they have no fucking clue what they're talking about. The whole thing is beyond frustrating. Addiction is pure fucking madness.

I haven't had a drink or a drug in almost twenty-three years, but I still have cravings. Maybe not for vodka or heroin anymore, but I do have cravings. I have cravings that could easily break the back of the strongest bull. I still have days where I need to take the day off and stay in bed. There are days when I wake up with cravings so strong that I don't even have the strength to stand up. This is very rare, but it happens. If you have been to a few twelve-step meetings already, you will hear people talk about their cravings for their drug of choice leaving them after working their twelve-step program thoroughly. Yes, their cravings for their drug of choice might have left them, but a lot of people won't tell you that their cravings have just slid over to something else.

Most people go straight to food after quitting drinking and drugs. You will see a lot of people gain a shit ton of weight after a few months of sobriety. Some people binge on exercise or yoga. Some people will dive into work. A lot of people will get into pornography. There are endless directions to go with addiction. A lot of people will never talk about their new addictions. Some won't even know that they have crossed over to something else. Remember, denial is a major side effect of the addict mind. Addicts lie a lot. We lie to other people, we lie to ourselves, and we'll lie to you. Just stick around, you'll see.

But in a way, this is all normal and par for the course for an addict. I'd say that 98% of us do this, and it's okay. It's part of recovery. True recovery from addiction takes years because we're not just recovering from some drug that brought us to our knees. Addiction isn't knowing we have a problem. Addiction is finding out we have a problem but not knowing how or even wanting to quit. Addiction is about being completely overwhelmed by life, wanting to hide and disappear. Addiction is about fucked-up families, not getting what we think we deserve out of life, and burning everything around us to the ground.

If you're sitting at a desk in a room that you share with someone else, and it's 3:00 in the morning or 3:00 in the afternoon, and you're filling out a recovery workbook, maybe you're thinking about all these things I'm saying. Maybe you're not. If you're in rehab right now, who knows what's going through your mind? But I guarantee that there are hundreds of rehabs around the country filled with people sitting at a desk just like the one you're sitting at, and they're having the exact same thoughts you're having. If you're in rehab right now, that's a good start. You're probably exactly where you need to be.

Sure, maybe you're from Salt Lake City, Utah, and you somehow wound up in Delray Beach, Florida, but don't feel bad. Delray Beach is the rehab capital of the world. A lot of people end up in Delray Beach. Just stay put. You might actually like it. Sun, sand, the beach at your fingertips. Granted, depending on which drug you're detoxing from, you might be in bed longer than you'd like, but at least you have something to look forward to. All jokes aside, I hope you make it. Sobriety can be a beautiful experience, and you deserve that.

If you can stay sober, one day at a time, hit meetings every day, and hopefully not freak out over the higher-power stuff, you will have a really good chance of making it to the next level. Surround yourself with people who give you good vibes. When you graduate from your rehab program, get into a sober living house and do the same thing there. Hit meetings, pray, meditate, and surround yourself with people who want to stay sober and who want the best for you. You can do this.

THE SPONSOR AND
SPONSEE RELATIONSHIP

If you're thinking about getting sober, if you're in a thirty-day rehab center, or if you're a couple of weeks into hitting AA meetings, I'm sure you've heard of a twelve-step sponsor. Or maybe you haven't. That's okay. It's all good, right? I'm here to walk you through all this.

First off, if you're new to sobriety, that makes you a future sponsee. The sponsee is the person looking for guidance in the wacky and magical world of recovery. As a sponsee, the less you know, the better. I recommend making the sponge your spirit animal for a while. Just be open to learning new things regarding recovery. The person who becomes your sponsor will help you through the steps. Helping you through the twelve steps is your sponsor's main job. Any questions you have about the steps or the literature—such as the Big Book, the 12x12, and a few other books—your sponsor should be able to help you with.

I want to make it clear right away that your sponsor is not your therapist. Your sponsor is also not your personal ATM machine, so don't ask him for money. Also, your sponsor is not there to help you with your girlfriend or boyfriend problems. If you're in the middle of a breakup, you will want to talk with your therapist about that. Remember, your sponsor's main focus is to help you navigate through the steps and your recovery. I'm sure over time, as you get to know your sponsor better, he will be open to broadening the topics you discuss, but in the beginning, just keep it simple. Focus on staying sober. You're not going to AA or other twelve-step meetings to meet women or men, and you're not there to network and find ways to make money.

As a sponsee, you will want to be aware of a few other things. Once you finally get a sponsor, if after a couple of weeks or even a couple of days, you feel that the person you're working with doesn't work for you, that's okay. One of two things could be happening. One, you might feel uncomfortable because you're newly sober, and everything feels strange in the beginning. This is normal. You just met somebody new, and they have agreed to work these twelve steps that you know nothing about, and you're going to be rehashing some extremely personal shit. Just let the guy you're working with know how you're feeling. When you have questions, just ask. Everything will be okay.

But there could be another reason you're feeling uncomfortable with the person who has agreed to sponsor you. Your sponsor might be a bit of a creep.

Maybe your sponsor gets off on bossing people around, and you're his next victim. The twelve-step recovery community is full of different kinds of people. Just like in the rest of your life, you will come across the good, bad, and ugly of people in recovery. Not everybody you meet is going to have the best of intentions. There's the possibility that your new sponsor is a less than awesome person. You have every right to let the person you're working with go. There's no law saying you have to work with the first sponsor you meet forever. Relationships of all types end every day. This is all just the nature of the beast when it comes to living life. And I'm not trying to make you paranoid; I'm just being honest with you.

In my twenty-plus years of sobriety, I have had five sponsors, and one of them ended up being a creeper. Four out of five ain't bad. If you're wondering how to find a good sponsor, I can help with that too. There's an easy list of do's and don'ts when it comes to finding a sponsor. I recommend going to meetings as much as possible and just listening to people speak. Who makes you feel good when they talk? When the Seventh Tradition portion of the meetings comes up, the secretary of the meeting is going to ask if anyone needs a sponsor. Raise your hand and let the group know you need one. If the secretary doesn't ask this question, just raise your hand during the meetings and introduce yourself. Let everyone know you're new and would like a sponsor. This is a great way to attract the right kind of person.

A good sponsor will have the ability to listen to you but also set healthy boundaries. It's important that both people are comfortable. A good sponsor knows that a newly sober person is going to be in a lot of pain. A lot of newly sober people will have a lot of fear and anger in the beginning. A good sponsor will be a patient person. I also want to make you aware that you might meet someone who agrees to work with you but changes their mind after a week. Maybe they have come to the realization that they're too busy. Maybe they just don't like you. This would be unfortunate, but it's a possibility. Don't let an experience like this deter you. Just keep moving forward. You will find someone who is right for you. Remember, addiction is all about fucked-up feelings that aren't real, so learning how not to take other people too personally will be a trick for you to learn.

The sponsor-sponsee relationship is one of the greatest relationships out there. A strong spiritual connection between two people is an amazing thing that very few people will ever get to experience. My hope is that anyone and everyone who has a strong desire to get sober is able to do just that. But sobriety and recovery are a strange kind of battle that takes place in the mind, and I'm convinced that finding someone to help you through that war is one of the best decisions someone trying to get sober can make.

I stayed sober for eight years without a higher power, without a twelve-step program, and without a sponsor, and it almost killed me. I was close to losing everything during those eight years. I lived in poverty, I had no friends or family to turn to, and I almost lost my mind. AA, my higher power, and my sponsors saved my life. It's that simple. I would be dead if it wasn't for those three things. If I come off like I'm trying to sell you this shit, I'm not. I'm not a company man by nature. There are things about the twelve-step community that turn me off. But overall, twelve-step recovery of any kind can be an amazing tool if used properly. All of these twelve-step programs were created and started by people inspired by a higher being, in my opinion. Recovery and the people in recovery are going to be messy at times. Addicts are sensitive, thin-skinned people with brains designed to make up stories that aren't true. When you put a bunch of people like that in a room together, life is going to get interesting. But if you stick with it, you're going to meet some amazing and interesting people. Some of them will become your friends.

So, if you're still wondering what you should do, if you're wondering which road to take, just take a left on Sobriety Lane, and go for it. You have already tried living life your way, and it hasn't been working, so try something new.

DRAMA IN THE ROOMS

One of the reasons I wanted to write this book is to create a third option for people who want to read about twelve-step meetings and recovery culture. Right now, there are only two camps to choose from. Camp number one is for the believers—people who need to drink the Kool-Aid and believe everything they read, hear, or see. They refuse to question anything once they've committed to a cause. Then you have camp number two: the haters, the devil's advocates, and the victims. You will find a lot of literature written by both camps. I want to write a book that talks about the good and not-so-good aspects of twelve-step meetings and recovery.

I believe AA and all the other twelve-step groups are rooted in wanting to help people. But people are complicated. Addiction is complicated. The human brain is fucking complicated. When you put a bunch of people in a room and have them spill their guts for three minutes, things are going to get weird. Then you add a higher power that can be a million different things to a million different people and have them read out of books written by other alcoholics from the 1930s—shit's going to get even more wonky. If you didn't know, Alcoholics Anonymous was started by a bunch of middle-aged white guys who grew up very religious and were chewed up and spit out by the military during World War I. A lot of these guys were beaten by their extremely religious fathers as children. They came from a generation that saw a lot of shit: war, the Dust Bowl, the Great Depression, you name it.

I'm sure these guys were Republicans, and I'm sure there was a lot of racism going on as well. People got married at seventeen, men drank and beat their wives and kids, and times were rough for everyone. I'm not saying that all white Republican men back in the day were racists who drank and beat their families, but this seems to be where the founders of Alcoholics Anonymous came from. Back then, this shit was normal. Yes, people still drink hard and hurt the ones they love, but now most of society knows that this is a bad thing.

I'm sitting here thinking, *What the hell can I say to the person reading this chapter?* I have already said many times that twelve-step meetings are a special thing. Meetings save lives. I have talked about how you will meet a lot of great people who will make your life so much better than when you were running amok. But I feel I would be doing you a disservice if I didn't mention the things that can go on in the circle of sobriety and recovery. Anybody and everybody that spends enough time in the rooms of twelve-step meetings is going to witness and eventually even be part of some drama. I'm guilty of pulling some shit myself. The drama is almost always caused by jealousy. And what's the jealousy all about? Simple. Dick and pussy. It doesn't matter what you're into. If you're a man who likes women, a man who likes other men, or a woman who hates men and just wants to scissor the shit out of some woman who only wants dick, somebody is going to want what somebody else has.

Of course, there will be people in the rooms who are mildly pissed at someone who seems to be living the easy life while they have to work like a dog and can barely afford a shitty studio apartment that always seems to smell like a kitty litter box even though they don't even own a fucking cat. But overall, people in the rooms of all these twelve-step meetings talk shit about each other because of dick and pussy. Ninety percent of all the people you will ever meet in a meeting will have the emotional intelligence of a fourteen-year-old. It doesn't matter if the person you meet is twenty-five or fifty-five. They're all insecure middle school children.

You might be confused by the things I'm saying. In one breath, I tell you that twelve-step meetings are amazing, beautiful places filled with amazing, beautiful people, and in the next breath, I rant about how most the people going to these meetings are insecure children who just want to dry hump everything in sight. Well, it's all true. This is what makes AA meetings, Al-Anon meetings, and all the recovery meetings out there so fucking wild. Being in recovery is like living in your very own pop art painting. Art is beauty, pain, violence, and love all rolled into one. Recovery is the same thing. One day you will be sitting in a meeting at 6:00 pm, and a beautiful woman will walk in. You have never seen her before, and the two of you will lock eyes. After the meeting, you might talk for a few minutes. Maybe you go on a coffee date. Two months later, you're moving in together. The sex is amazing, the conversation is great, and you can't imagine being with anyone else. Two months after that, you come home, and your locks have been changed, and all your clothes are in the hallway. Who knows why this happened? You're going to say she's crazy, and she's going to say that you're a piece of shit. Again, you're both right. She's crazy, and you are most likely a total piece of shit. But we will never get the whole story from either one of you because you're both addicts. You like booze, and she likes being with guys who are into booze and are not emotionally available. You're both love addicts, and that's what you have in common. Hey, man, this happens every ninety seconds in recovery.

When it's not happening to you, it's kind of entertaining, but when it does finally happen to you, watch out, boy. Grab your balls, change all your passwords to everything, make sure your bank accounts are in order, and just lay low for a month or so. Let it all blow over. The last thing you want to do is piss off a codependent love addict with borderline personality disorder. Someone with those kinds of problems will make it their new full-time job to destroy your life in every way imaginable. I have gone through this twice in my life, and each time was horrifying. Granted, I might have deserved a little of what I got, but shit, let a dying dog lie. I hope I used that reference correctly. Probably not.

Look, the point to all this is, yes, go to meetings, make friends, work with your sponsor, but for God's sake, don't fuck everything that moves. In the beginning, most addicts don't know the difference between sex and love. I know I didn't. Take advantage of everything that recovery and the twelve-step programs have to offer, but don't go too far. Isn't that what we addicts do? Taking things too far is our specialty. But when does it stop? I don't think we know when it stops. That's why we go to meetings. So do that. Just go to meetings. Keep your dicks and your pussies in your pants for a year or so, and just pray to God you can make it that long.

LITTLE SAIGON

A lot of people in recovery think it's their environment that plays the biggest role in whether they stay sober or not. I'm here to tell you that's bullshit. It doesn't matter if you grew up rich or poor. It doesn't matter if you spent your youth living in a mansion in Beverly Hills or in a trailer park in West Virginia. Addiction is everywhere. Addiction doesn't care where you come from.

As I write this, fentanyl is destroying entire neighborhoods in San Francisco, Philadelphia, and Baltimore. Everybody in Portland and Nashville is stoned out of their minds, and Miami will always be ground zero for cocaine. Florida has more opiate addicts than the rest of the U.S. states combined, and one out of every five homes in Delray Beach, Florida, is a sober living facility. And if you want meth, Fresno, California, and anywhere in Michigan, Indiana, or Missouri are definitely the places for you. In my personal experience, the most alcoholic town I have ever been to is Anchorage, Alaska, hands down. There's something special going on in Alaska that makes some of the people living there especially dark and violent when alcohol is added to their system.

Look, my point is that—and I have said this a million times to people in person and in my past work—no matter where you are, addiction and any kind of drug will find you if you want it to. I have found drugs out in the middle of the California desert. I have run into people with booze and heroin while camping out in the middle of nowhere in Washington State, Alaska, Oregon, and Montana. I don't need to be in Manhattan, Downtown LA, or San Francisco's Tenderloin District if I want easy access to the street version of a twenty-four-hour pharmacy. And this isn't happening just in the United States. Mexico, Sweden, Germany, Russia, anywhere in Asia—you can find whatever you want, whenever you want. The whole world is open for business. So, when I hear some dude in an AA meeting cry about all the stupid reasons why he relapsed and how he might not have relapsed if he'd grown up in a nicer house or if his parents loved him more or if his priest never touched him inappropriately, it's all bullshit. You can grow up in Santa Barbara, have loving parents, go on beautiful vacations, go to the best schools, and have the prettiest wife or the richest husband, and you can still find a way to fuck it all up.

What does this mean? It means that the guy who woke up today on the corner of 4th and Davis in Portland's Oldtown neighborhood, dope sick and getting rained on, has just as much of a chance of getting sober as some spoiled twenty-four-year-old who just woke up in a cozy bed at Cliffside Malibu Treatment Center. Whether you want to call them sick or you want to call them the family fuckups, they're equals on day one.

The best advice I can give to someone trying to get sober is to kill your bullshit script. It doesn't matter why you drank or used drugs. It doesn't matter how much you used in the past. Neither addiction nor sobriety or recovery cares about what you used to do for work or what your parents or grandparents do or did for work. Only people are impressed by another person's position in life or lack thereof. If you're trying to get sober and want to stay sober long-term, I recommend that you erase everything you think you know. You don't know shit. Sobriety isn't college. Sobriety isn't ordering things online and having those things delivered to your doorstep. Sobriety and recovery take the kind of work that eats lazy people for breakfast. I think one of the reasons so many more people are relapsing now than ever is because the average person today is just so much softer than the first generation of people trying to get sober back in the late 1930s. I think all the technology and inventions that make our lives easier have made so many of us complete pansies. Cancel culture, this new woke far-left shit, the new education system from kindergarten all the way up to graduating college has fucked people up. YouTube is filled with videos of people having nervous breakdowns because a coworker was mean to them at work. Are you fucking kidding me?

I remember back in 2016, when Trump became president, I was at an AA meeting, and a young woman in her early thirties raised her hand to share and started bawling and freaking out about Trump becoming president. I saw this woman at least three times a week at meetings for about a year. I have not seen her since that night she shared. What the fuck? If all it takes is Donald Trump to cause you to relapse, you're in serious trouble. What are you going to do when someone close to you passes away? What happens if you get fired from your dream job or if anything else really important happens? Are you just going to call up your dealer or walk to whatever corner you walk to and pick up your go-to baggie of death that you love so much? Every time someone looks at you the wrong way, or the line at Trader Joe's is too long, or you get stood up on yet another Tinder date, are you going to drink, smoke, snort, and shoot your life away? What's the point in that?

I ask these questions because everything I'm saying will happen. I guarantee it. Poor or rich, shitty things happen to everyone. This is why we go to meetings. This is why we get a sponsor. This is why we share what is going on with us in the meetings. This is why we do everything that we do. Because, for most of us, if we don't do these things, we too will relapse. Our lives will turn to shit. You aren't special. This shit doesn't just happen to you. These things happen to every addict—lawyer, doctor, teacher, grocery clerk, mailman, welder, fisherman, and eighteen-year-old who just inherited $6.5 million from their dead grandfather who invested in Microsoft back in 1975. Bad things happen to everyone, especially addicts. Addicts tend to make more stupid decisions than the average person. I think it's just a side effect of the disease. Lucky us, right? For me, if I go too long without talking to my sponsor, I do tend to start making more bad decisions. If I only go to one AA meeting a week, eventually I start to get bitchy. I lose my patience with people quicker. The asshole in me comes out much more regularly. This is just how I'm wired. This is how most addicts are wired. Again, this is why we do what we do.

Look, I would love to live in a posh condo in my neighborhood of choice. I would love to make more money, and I would love more free time so I could travel more. I get it. I want things too. I get jealous of people who have the shit I want. Sometimes I get pissed off when I talk to someone who seems to have it all. I get all this shit all too well. I just moved into the Little Saigon neighborhood, which is a two-block neighborhood inside San Francisco's Tenderloin. I'll be the first to tell you that it's not ideal, but I want to save money on rent, so I found the cheapest place I could find to save that money.

I have been here for two weeks now, and I have already seen countless overdoses as I walk out my front gate. I just found out four nights ago that my building has a major rat infestation, and, lucky me, it's my job to solve this problem because I manage the building I live in. I have seen four rats that are roughly the size of a three-week-old pit bull puppy. These rats are fucking huge, and they have been in control of the building I live in for too long. The woman who lives above me is a crack and meth addict, and she screams and yells at her live-in boyfriend and her two small dogs. This woman is a true psychopath, and it's my job to get her out of the building. I knew things were going to get weird by moving into this building, but you never know how weird things are going to get until you pull the trigger and move in. Am I crazy for doing this? Maybe. But I'm an addict, so in a way, it makes sense. On the plus side, my neighborhood and the Tenderloin have given me so much material to use for my writing. I have written more in the past month than I have in the past five months. I seem to be more plugged in with my creativity when I live in a shitty neighborhood that might kill me. I guess a little fear never hurts anybody.

Just the other night, I was smoking a cigar outside my building, and I ended up chatting with five guys smoking crack. I played The Beatles while we talked outside, and I just watched dozens of people come and go, cross the street, buy their drugs, smoke their drugs, and take turns walking in circles, falling down, and just staying down. I live in the center of a zombie apocalypse right now. I have lived in this before, but it doesn't affect me the way it used to. I don't take what is happening in my neighborhood personally like I did the last time I lived here. The drugs, the death, the giant rats, and the woman above me have nothing to do with me. None of this is my fault. And I don't have to drink or use because of any of this. I won't use because of any of this. I'm more powerful than any ghetto. I'm stronger than the junkies who crawl around my sidewalk looking for the drugs they think they lost. Fuck those giant dog-sized rats in my building's basement. I'm going to take care of those things sooner rather than later.

Most problems have an answer, and I have some of the answers needed to solve a few of the problems I've listed. Once you have the answers, all you need is time, and I have time. At least I hope I do. If you're reading this, you have time too. And even if you don't have a lot of time left, at least you have the choice to spend what time you have left making better decisions. Whatever problems you have, there's someone out there who has the answers for you. You just have to reach out. I hope you do.

ART AND RECOVERY

I've been listening to Miles Davis's *Bitches Brew* album all day today, and it hit me: Where would we be without art? Life would be so empty without musicians, painters, writers, and dancers. I spend so much of my days and nights listening to music. Maybe it's to distract me from certain bad feelings or stave off boredom. Or maybe The Beatles make me feel good. Maybe Pink Floyd will take me to another place that I wouldn't normally go if it weren't for their music. In my experience, Sade takes kissing an attractive woman to a sexier place than I could take it on my own. Food and music. Sex and music. Breakup songs. Getting-back-together songs. Most of us have experienced these things, right? I know I have. To this day, listening to "Lady in Red" makes me sad because it reminds me of my ex-fiancé. Once in a blue moon, I still listen to that song because a part of me enjoys being sad while reminiscing about Nicole.

When I first got sober, I was too afraid to go out at night, so I would just stay home and watch movies. I've probably seen *Jaws* a hundred times by now. That movie always took my mind off wanting to drink. For years, I would watch three, sometimes four movies a night. I would usually start with a comedy like *Planes, Trains, and Automobiles* and then go to a more action-packed flick like *Die Hard*. Then I'd go for some straight horror like *Friday the 13*th or *Halloween*. To close out the night, around 2:00 in the morning, I'd watch something slower, maybe a small-budget indie film like *Clerks*.

When I first got off all the booze and drugs, I couldn't be around people outside of work for a while, so film and music became my buddies. Depending on my mood, I would watch certain movies or listen to specific bands. Pink Floyd's *Wish You Were Here* album helped me get past missing my mother. I can't count how many hours of house music I've listened to while working out or jogging. And then there's all the ambient and classical music that goes perfectly with meditation. No matter the mood or situation, there's a song for it.

One of my favorite hobbies is thinking about songs that would go perfectly with moments I've already experienced or for a future situation that could come my way. What would be the best song for that moment I ask my future fiancé to marry me? What time of day would it be? Where would this take place? Every detail matters. If it's late at night, you just got done salsa dancing, and you're in Rio de Janeiro, you might want to hear Sade's "By Your Side." Or it could be early in the day, you're spending the weekend in a log cabin somewhere in Colorado, so maybe Bonnie Raitt's "I Can't Make You Love Me" would be more suitable.

In recovery, I've come across so many creative people. I've met dancers, musicians, painters, and writers at AA meetings over the years. I think addiction and creativity go hand in hand. The more brilliant the artist, the more fucked up they seem to be. To this day, I've never met an artist who didn't have some kind of battle with depression and anxiety. Personally, I feel like I'm plugged into something that I cannot fully explain, so I chase it with my writing. Whether the writing is good or not doesn't really matter to me. I just need to get "it" out. If I didn't have my writing, I think I would emotionally implode. I know other artists who feel the same way I do.

I've had some amazing conversations after a meeting while visiting places like Los Angeles and New York. I always love going to those cities because they have the best AA meetings. Some of the most interesting people I've ever met have been in some random church basement or a meeting space connected to a Bank of America. One minute you're at an AA meeting, and the next thing you know, you're talking to the bass player of some amazing band you grew up listening to. Or a guy will walk up to you, and it turns out he was one of the leading graphic artists back in the late '80s and used to sell coke to Duran Duran. I love that shit, and it's part of the reason why I keep coming back to meetings. You never know who you're going to meet.

I love talking about the thin line between brilliance and insanity. Mental illness versus mental breakthrough. I love talking about living on that edge. And not because you want to, but because that's how you're wired. It's not a choice. You just have to make the best of it. Create or be destroyed. It's very rare when I meet someone who gets what I mean by this, but when I do, I know I'm not crazy. Hell no. I'm a fucking artist. You might be too. If you're reading this and lights are popping off in your head, you definitely should be creating something regularly. Maybe you already are, but if you aren't, I hope you find your creative calling. There are so many avenues to go down when it comes to art, and it's almost endless. And once you find your fix, life is going to get that much better. I guarantee it!

IN A SILENT WAY

Do you pray? The first time I really prayed was in 2012. I was still living in Portland, Oregon, and I walked into the First Congregational United Church of Christ on SW Park and Madison. I had walked by that church a million times over the years, so I decided to go in. It was always open, and people were always coming and going, so I thought, why not?

As soon as I walked in, I was immediately drawn to these gigantic dark brown doors. I walked through the doors expecting to enter a large ornate room, but it turned out to be a very small room with a few chairs and some stained-glass windows. So, I sat down, closed my eyes, and quietly said, "God, can you hear me?" This was, after all, the first time I had ever truly attempted to pray. Part of me was afraid a loud voice would tell me to leave the room. I didn't know whose loud voice it would be, but I expected to be thrown out. But nothing happened. So, I sat quietly for a few minutes. I didn't know what to do. Eventually, I said, "God, please help me. I'm a fucking loser. I need help. I don't know how to achieve anything. I don't even know what I want. Please help me not be such a fuck-up. Amen."

And that was my first prayer. I had been meditating for years at that point, but I didn't feel like I was getting anywhere. My sponsor kept telling me that praying helped him, but I refused to do it. I couldn't pray. I didn't believe in God. But something changed when I asked God to help me stop being such a fucking loser. Just like the day I decided to stop drinking, I felt something. The day I decided to quit drinking and using, I felt something, and the day I finally decided to pray, I felt something very similar again. Each time, it was as if something had touched the center of my forehead. It was as if someone had said, "Let it be so." I have never questioned what happened on those days. It is what it is.

So now I pray. I pray all the time. And I believe in God. Not because I want to. It's just the way it is.

SOMETIMES THINGS GET WORSE BEFORE THEY GET BETTER?

When I decided to get sober back in 2001, I was just twenty-two years old. No more booze, heroin, cigarettes, Ecstasy, or any of the other garbage I put into my body regularly. I thought that was all it would take for my life to turn around. But things became much darker for a while. Not all addicts are the same, but for a lot of us, quitting all the junk is just the first layer of the onion in our life transformation. A whole new adventure lies ahead, and none of us are even remotely prepared for what happens next.

You see, at the beginning of my using career, I thought I was drinking and taking drugs to have fun. I wanted to take the good times up a few notches. A lot of us start this way. Why just go to a party and drink beer when you can go to a party, take some LSD, take a few shots of vodka, and then pop some kind of pill at two in the morning that will keep you up for sixteen more hours? That makes total sense to me. Maybe it makes sense to you as well. Those nights were always a blast for me. At times I miss nights like those. The part I don't miss is partying in Portland, Oregon, and waking up broke, missing my ID and credit cards, and somehow stranded in Seattle. How the fuck did that happen? And how was I supposed to get home?

Once I quit using, I thought my life would get better right away. But that didn't happen. The truth is that when I first got sober, I didn't really have much to offer the world. I hadn't gone to college yet, and the only jobs I had were being a male model, a drug dealer, and working at Starbucks and a couple of nightclubs. I'd always been paid under the table, usually in the form of drugs. I can remember living with my grandmother, borrowing money for the bus, and filling out job applications at Target, random grocery stores, and, of course, the infamous Cinnabon Bakery. Eventually, this small café with a flower shop in Portland hired me for seven bucks an hour. The owners hated me right away because I was unable to take simple verbal instructions. I didn't know it at the time, but alcohol and drugs had really fucked up my head. I could barely make coffee. When my manager talked to me, half the time I spaced out thinking about nothing. I couldn't focus on anything for the next two years. After a few months, I got fired for the same reasons most newly sober people get fired: because most newly sober people are borderline useless.

I took jobs at a couple of gyms so I could work out for free, and then I found a job at a tile factory selling floor tile that people had brought back from jobs and didn't need anymore. My department was called the Seconds Department. Of course it was. The Seconds Department was filled with guys like me: young, uneducated, and probably going nowhere. But on the plus side, I was able to get a little studio in Northwest Portland. Finally, things were starting to get better. I stayed at the tile job for two years until one day I was cleaning out a giant 8,000-square-foot basement and realized that I had to make a major change. After cleaning out that basement for a month straight, I told my boss I was going to college. He laughed at me. But I did go back to college.

What drove me even more to go back to college than cleaning out that fucking basement was the voice of my mother telling me when I was twenty-one that I would never go to college. I had to show my mother that I could make something out of my life. I didn't know how long it was going to take, but eventually, it would happen.

After a couple of years, I learned that college was a good investment, but it wouldn't guarantee me success. I learned that college is nothing more than a place to meet people and show a future employer that you can stick with something for a while. Outside of this, college for some people could be a total waste of time. If you know what you want to do with your life, you might as well just focus on that thing. But at the time, I had no idea what I wanted to do. I knew I wanted to be a famous actor or rock star, but pursuing fame for a newly sober junkie isn't the best idea. I knew I needed a few more opportunities, and college was the only thing I knew that might give me those opportunities. I briefly thought about joining the army, but I had a feeling boot camp would drive me insane. I think going from being a drug addict and alcoholic to being in the military is just too much of a change. Or maybe it would have been the best thing for me at the time. We will never know because I didn't go.

But enough of my bullshit. What about you? How are things for you? Is this your first day sober? Are you a couple of months in? A year in? How is life going for you? Is it amazing? Is it all you dreamed it would be? Or are you struggling? Depression? Anxiety? Has a doctor given you the dreaded bipolar diagnosis?

Over the years, I have met many people in the rooms that are dual diagnosis, which basically means an addict with another separate mental illness. In my case, I'm a recovering addict and alcoholic with clinical depression and general anxiety disorder. This might be one of the most common dual diagnoses out there in the twelve-step community. But you will meet a lot of people with bipolar 1 and 2, schizoaffective disorder, and borderline personality disorder, which seems to be popular these days.

I don't think enough people talk about their dual diagnosis issues in the rooms, which is why there's still a bit of a stigma in the rooms and in society as a whole. When people tell the truth and talk about what's really going on, light can be brought to many topics that are usually difficult for the public to speak about and hear. I know so many people in my AA meetings that are obviously dealing with mental health issues beyond their addiction, but they refuse to seek help because they're afraid. Afraid of what? Well, I think people are afraid of being pushed into an undesirable category.

If you're a man and on a first date with an attractive woman, and she tells you that she's nine months sober and has bipolar 2 disorder, what is your first reaction? I'll tell you my first reaction. Run! Get the fuck out of that restaurant because eventually that woman is going to ruin your life. If you have any common sense, this will be your first reaction. Or if you're in a job interview and the person interviewing you sees that you have had six jobs in the past two years, that is a big red flag to the interviewer. And why have you switched jobs so many times? Oh, you have a slight meth problem, and you keep spazzing out at the company parties and getting fired the following Monday? How do you tell a possible future employer that? You can be sober for years, but your past can still come back to bite you on the ass without a moment's notice.

And now that we have social media, we're even more fucked. We can't get away with anything anymore. There are some things that we do that can never be undone. Maybe we have changed. Maybe we're better people today, but in the eyes of some people, a lot of people, time doesn't matter. Once a thief, always a thief, right? Addiction can be the gift that keeps on giving for some of us.

But one other thing I love about the rooms of twelve-step meetings is that over time, we can show each other that we have changed. Along the way, someone will see your change and appreciate what you have become, and that person might know someone who could use someone like you in their company. Yes, we don't go to meetings to find jobs, but these are programs of attraction, and when we do good things, over time, we will attract good things. We will be given gifts such as a better job or a new romantic partner. We don't know how or why, but good things happen. And all you have to do is focus on your sobriety. You just have to do the next right thing. It's very simple.

So, if you're a drunk or an addict or both or if you're an addict with a mood disorder, it's not the end of the world. Just find a way to stay sober and get to those meetings. Tell people what's really going on with you. Work those steps and read those damn books. Good things will happen. Most likely not as fast as you'd like them to, but good things will happen. The only thing that will make things worse for you is hiding. Not letting people in is a death sentence for a real addict. Whenever I cut people out of my life, things just turn to shit for me. And as soon as I let people back in, my life gets better. And that's saying a lot because I'm a total introvert who loves my alone time. But I do want to live, so I force myself to do all the things that I mention in this book. Sometimes being around people can feel painful for me, but afterward, I always feel a little better. If you're in the fight for your life and struggling with addiction and you want to live, I recommend you at least try these things. How much worse could it get, right?

DUANE'S OPINION

When: 8:00 pm, 5.10.24
Where: 829 Folsom
What: Interview with Duane

Duane is the first person I met when I moved to San Francisco from Key West. He wasn't the first person I met in a San Francisco AA meeting. No, Duane was the first person I talked to in San Francisco. I went to a noon AA meeting at the Dry Dock, and Duane introduced himself to me. Duane looked like the kind of guy that Jack Kerouac would have hung around with back in the 1950s. He's about my age, very lean, about five foot seven, and always looks like he just got back from a six-month sea voyage. Permanently unshaven, in a white T-shirt and gray sweatpants, Duane is one of my favorite people in San Francisco. He's always ready to help you in any way he can, and he doesn't lie. He's just like me in that he doesn't know how to lie to people. This can be a good thing, but it can also be a bad thing. We both could have saved ourselves a lot of heartache if we had just told a few well-placed lies in our lifetime. But like I said, Duane and I don't lie.

Duane has seen a lot in a short amount of time. He has lived a fast life, drunk, and drugged just as much as anyone else out there. Well-traveled, married too young, small businesses come and gone, divorced young, and always trying to find his way—Duane has always wanted to live a simple life with no drama, and I've always found his journey toward this life to be fascinating.

A few days ago, I asked Duane if I could interview him for this book, and of course, he said yes. I really want to get Duane's perspective on recovery, twelve-step meetings, and the overall culture of Alcoholics Anonymous. Here's what Duane had to say.

***

Mark: "So, Duane, how do you want to begin this? Where do you want to start?"

Duane: "When I first got here."

Mark: "Okay, start with that, and just start telling the story."

Duane: "Okay, so I met up with this guy who ended up being my sponsor. He says, 'Okay, Duane, you need to start going to these meetings. Why don't you just start going to the Dry Dock? There are so many meetings there.' So, I started going in there. I was going in there at 6:00 am all the way up 'til 10:00 at night. At the time, there seemed to be meetings every hour. It was just an endless cycle of different types of people that I was starting to see. I also wanted to see how these people acted when they weren't drinking, you know.

"At first, I was really cagey, like I am normally in society. I'm a really cagey person. I'll keep it cool; I'll keep things under wraps with people. I'm very wary of other people's privacy. I try to keep a low profile with other people in general. But I started opening up to some of these older guys in the rooms, and their common interests seemed to match mine. They didn't want to drink, they wanted to go to as many meetings as I did, they did everything that's suggested, and most of all, they participated in life. That was, and still is to this day, the thing that I'm hungry for. Any aspect of my life, I want to be there, and I want to help other people when I can. When I was drinking, I wasn't like this. I wasn't participating in life.

"After a while, I started to see some of the signs I wasn't warned about. Like, I was on day five of my sobriety, and I met a lady who was in Al-Anon, and it says we're not really supposed to do anything for the first year, but well, on day five I was dealing with a chick in Al-Anon. Some of the older guys pulled me aside and said, 'Hey Duane, you gotta watch this kind of behavior because sometimes it can go south. Shit can get crazy.'

"At this time, I was on a downward direction. Luckily, these two ladies from the Dry Dock invited me on a picnic over at Crissy Field to kind of lighten me up a little bit. After that picnic, something really cool happened. I started engaging with the Dry Dock folks again and just tried to figure something out. The program talks about all these 'isms,' why people use, all the slogans which are great for like a cheat sheet for not drinking. But when it all comes down to it, when they say, build a new life, build relationships with people, I've built some solid relationships with some people in the program. For me, I like to go to meetings at places like the Dry Dock to practice for society. Engaging with people at meetings helps me behave in a better way out in the world. So, in terms of society, I'm a decent person because of the Dry Dock.

"I think a lot of times, what people don't understand is that someone who's going through injuries, who's using drugs in the emergency room as prescribed, not drinking, you know, the meetings help in general. But for me, the Dry Dock has a spiritual value that a lot of other places don't. Once you find a place that really works for you, you gotta stay with it. Don't take it for granted.

"When I was a kid, I grew up watching these horror movies. Somebody is in their deepest, darkest moment in the basement of some house getting chased by something, and they find a way to break through. They find a way out of that house. That feeling that person gets when they know they're free, that's what the Dry Dock is for me. The Dry Dock is that feeling for me. It's a place for me to break out of myself, be around people who have a common problem and want to be free like I do. You know, going into the Dry Dock is like going into an X-ray machine. You're going to find out who you are. You're going to find out who everybody else is. There are going to be things that are going to go around that you're going to have to deal with. The harassment, people's opinions, people bringing in their outside issues—people are going to do these things all the time, no matter where you go to meetings. We're all human, man. There's good and bad in all areas of our lives.

"I sponsor two guys out of the Dock currently. I make sure they're going to meetings. I'm not really a hardcore sponsor. I might give you a reading assignment, give you something to see what you do with it. I've met the hardcore guys, and most of them are nice individuals, but they do that because that works for them. I just go to the Dock because it works for me. I go there, I get together with some of the people, I eat with them there, go to holiday events. It's how I fill some of the voids I have. My family lives over 2,000 miles away, so I don't get to see them as often as I would like. The Dry Dock helps with that.

"I heard some of the tales of the Dock and how it used to be during its glory days. I think for the most part, man, I want to be a part of that building's future. I don't know, man. It's like I said earlier. It has that spiritual value. You know, we go in there, it's not like it's a church or nothing, you know. It takes me back to when I was a kid. I had a friend who invited me to church. It was this small white building. It looked like a small house. We went in there, and everybody was taking cross-shaped cookie cutters and cutting up these small pieces of dough that were going to harden up, and they were going to put them in the oven. We were making cross cookies. The Dry Dock reminds me of that place and those simple times. I like the simpler times, and I miss them. The Dry Dock gives me back those simpler times.

"Another thing I love about the Dock is that you get to meet people from all over the world who are just stopping by to get their meeting fix. You know, writers, actors, professional boxers, all walks of life, right? Yeah, you get to meet everybody."

Mark: "Let's say you and I were invited to go talk to somebody at a rehab center. Like somebody asks us to come talk to this kid, Mike. He's struggling and he'd like to talk to a couple of guys, and we go in there, and he asks us, 'What's it like to go to AA meetings? I've never been to an AA meeting before. I have to start going to AA meetings because of all this shit I did, but I don't know what to expect. What can I expect?' What would you say to some twenty-four-year-old kid with seventeen days sober who has never experienced recovery or AA before?"

Duane: "Well, I'd tell him, check it out. Those seventeen days that you have, what did it take to get there? It took you a day at a time, right? Well, why not try this other thing a day at a time, and if you don't like it, you're free to try out another meeting or you're free to sit back in your misery."

Mark: "I've also been thinking about how back when Covid was going on and everything was shut down, all these older guys in their late fifties, sixties, and seventies, with twenty-plus years clean, were relapsing. Even worse, some guys were relapsing and even committing suicide. A lot of people we knew relapsed during Covid. So, let's say we're at an AA meeting, anywhere, and this random guy who's fifty-five years old with twenty years of solid sobriety admits in the meeting that he's struggling, he's depressed, his wife is leaving him, and his kids won't talk to him anymore. Most people think this is the shit that happens to you before you get sober. It's not supposed to happen to someone who has a ton of time clean. What would you say to a guy like this? This guy just told a room full of people that he's fucked and he wants to drop out of recovery. What would you say?"

Duane: "Well, a guy like that? Well, here's the thing. You can't put anything in front of your recovery. Recovery comes first, no matter what. But, when you lose things in your life, it might not be you. It may just be the people. Maybe they just grew tired of you. You never know. Okay, I just don't want to talk to this person anymore. It doesn't mean you did a bunch of things wrong. And it doesn't mean that you did all that program work for nothing either. You did all that work to get to that point, sober. Okay. Do you get me? And what comes next in your life is your next test. Say everything's going well for me right now.

Got the job, got the place, I got it going on. Some shit goes down, and I lose something that's sacred and true to me. I think rather than writing myself a shitty note and putting it in my shoes and jumping off the Golden Gate Bridge, I would rather call somebody that I know knows what I'm going through. I would rather call that person. That's gonna lead to either someone talking to me and helping me off the ledge or someone agreeing to meet me somewhere and talking about what's going on. I think the common thing missing with all these guys falling like flies is they didn't call someone. It's that fucking easy, man. If those guys would have made a call, I bet you they'd still be around today, unless it was their time to go, then that's a whole other story, right?

"You can be going through some real heavy shit, but if you make that phone call, you might figure some of it out. Chances are the person on the other end of that call has been there. They have been through something similar. There's a good chance that person has also thought about taking their life. Maybe their family left them. They lost a job. Fuck it, man, they have been there. I can't stress it enough. Make that fucking call, man. I think another thing that pushes people back to the drink is that they refuse to revisit old shit. For whatever reason, they don't think they need to. But we have to reface shit sometimes. It's like Doc Brown picks us up in that DeLorean time machine, and Doc Brown fucking says, 'All right, look, Duane, you're going to visit some shit you fucked up, but nobody's gonna know you fucked anything up. But you're gonna know how everything is gonna go down. So are you gonna be a dumbass and just fucking drink on me again, or are you gonna do the right thing?' Simple as that. You know, we're sitting there a lot of times in life, and we're teeter-tottering with the fucking guys or gals on our shoulders telling us whatever things we think we want to hear. I guess what I'm trying to say is that life brings you setbacks. But that's all they are, setbacks. It's not worth drinking over.

"At the end of the day, the recommendations and suggestions and advice that you would give a new guy with three days isn't any different than the guy with thirty years. What, do you think the guy that relapses with thirty years has a better, deeper reason for relapsing than the guy with three days? Fuck no! It's all bullshit, man. It's like getting tattoos. My reason for getting a tattoo is no better than yours. There's no good reason to get a tattoo, but we still get 'em. You've got 'em, I've got 'em, and everybody we know has 'em. It's all silly. Well, it's the same thing with reasons to relapse."

Mark: "It's almost like we're all Uncle Scrooge. Everybody that goes into AA or any twelve-step program is Uncle Scrooge, and they have to go see the ghosts of Christmas past, present, and future in order to get their lives right."

Duane: "We gotta!"

Mark: "You know what I mean? It's like we're all Bill Murray in the movie *Scrooged*."

Duane: "Yes! Your life is like a movie. You've got the year you were born, your production date, you've got the dash, and you've got your question mark. The question mark is just the inevitable, your death."

Mark: "Yeah."

Duane: "But in between that dash, what are you gonna fill it up with?"

Mark: "Yeah, that's good. Let's stop there, Duane. This was awesome. Thank you for stopping by and doing this with me. You rock!"

Duane: "Hell yeah, brother. Good luck, everybody!"

THE EMOTIONAL HANGOVER

In the program, so much focus is on the work we do to stay sober—admitting that we're powerless over drugs and alcohol, getting a sponsor, working the steps, having a spiritual experience, and then passing on the message. Helping another person is what this is all about, right? But getting from A to B, or steps one through twelve, takes time and energy. There's a lot of fear in doing things that are uncomfortable. While we're going to meetings, meeting with sponsors and sponsees, and learning how to tell the truth, many of us have jobs and families. Most of us don't have the luxury of taking a year off and devoting all our time to a twelve-step program. Many of us are going to work and trying to keep our relationships with our loved ones together while also trying to stay sober and work on our programs. This is a lot of work. It's important work. If we want to keep the good lives we currently have or try to rebuild the life we once had, we have a long road ahead of us. Hours will turn into days. Days will turn into months, and months will turn into years.

In those years, we will experience so much. Everyone around us will experience a lot of new things as well. Our friends and families will see our mood swings. They will wonder why we want to stay in bed for days. The thing about recovery that all addicts experience is that to move past our old habits, we will have to experience a kind of death. Our old ways and the person we used to be will need to die. Making this decision and going through the process of this kind of death is traumatizing. So, once you get over the habit of using drugs and alcohol, now you have this new trauma experience that you had no idea was coming your way. You didn't know this was going to happen, so how would your wife or husband know? Everybody thought you would get better after a few months. But the journey you're now on is going to take years. In all honesty, this is the journey of a lifetime.

Throughout this journey, you may lose some people you thought would be with you for many more years to come. But you will also make new relationships with people you never expected to come across. Some friendships will have to end. What used to work for you and some people in your life today may not work in the near future. The girlfriend who tried to take care of you those past couple of your using years may end up leaving you six months after you get out of rehab. Or maybe you will leave her. You might find that staying with the woman you thought was helping you was actually enabling your drug and alcohol use. Maybe she needed someone to

THANK YOU FOR SHARING

take care of, and as soon as you started to get better, the attraction she once had for you is gone because you no longer need a nurse.

If you decide to stay sober, over time, you're going to learn more about denial and codependency. Once you can see your old behaviors and the behaviors of the people around you for what they are, you will start to see who you should keep and who you should get rid of. When you get to this point, you will realize that you're becoming emotionally sober. Emotional sobriety is the main goal once you get over your physical need for your drug of choice. The funny thing about emotional sobriety is that we don't all achieve it. The alternative to emotional sobriety is being a dry drunk, which is someone who doesn't drink but still acts like an asshole regularly. The goal is to be as emotionally sober as possible. We're all human, and we all experience shitty days. Life happens. We have already established this. But if we follow the twelve steps and speak honestly with the people around us, it will help us stay emotionally sane. Our chances of getting into arguments with strangers, getting fired from jobs, cheating on our partners, and just acting like a fool are greatly reduced.

The worst thing I experience in my recovery is the dreaded emotional hangover. I have a hard time balancing all aspects of my life. There are some things that I like to fit into my weekly routine, and when I can't fit everything in, usually due to lack of energy, I tend to get down on myself. I'm a perfectionist. Most addicts are perfectionists. If I can't hit the gym at least three days a week, I feel like a lazy piece of shit. If I don't go to the number of AA meetings that I feel is acceptable, I feel like I'm not working a strong enough program. If I don't write a chapter a day, five days a week, I feel that I'm failing as an artist. This is what I struggle with, and I'm only using it as an example to prove that I'm only human, and I'm trying my best. Emotional hangover and mental burnout—these are real things that we all experience. But as a recovering addict, we need to pay special attention to these things. Monitoring how we feel throughout the day will save our lives. Getting enough sleep, drinking water throughout the day, maintaining a healthy diet, exercising, surrounding ourselves with good people who want the best for us and vice versa—these are all so important for us. These things will help us stay sober.

And there's nothing wrong with feeling shitty. We're not weak for crying in the shower and not knowing where the tears came from. We all need to realize that we just got done drinking for the past ten or twenty years. Some of us smoked meth half our lives or shot up dope. We're going to be a bit loony for a while. For a long while, actually. Our brains and bodies need time to learn how to live and react to the world around us without the medicine we used to take every day. This adjustment period is going to be exhausting for us in the recovery game. Knowing this, I have to remind myself and everyone taking the recovery journey to be kind to us and to be kind to ourselves.

Yes, we have all made some big mistakes. We have done a lot of harm, not only to others but to ourselves over the years. To become healthy, we must forgive ourselves. And if the people around us cannot forgive us, we must accept that. Maybe some of them will come around. Maybe not. But we must move forward. Allow yourself to go through everything that comes your way. The exhaustion, the depression, the mood swings, and the negative self-talk—it's all coming, whether we like it or not. But the reason for this book is to tell you the truth, help prepare you, and help you become the person you want to be. I'm not here to sell you happiness. I'm not going to tell you how to make a million dollars because I don't know how to make a million dollars yet. But I do want to see you get sober. I want to see you and everyone trying to get sober achieve that goal. I know how to stay sober, and staying sober is what this book is about.

RELIGION VS. SPIRITUALITY
VS. THE ATHEIST

Let's talk more about God. Why not, right? I feel that there has always been quite a bit of tension in the twelve-step community regarding God, religion, and spirituality. Many people have strong feelings when it comes to these topics. Some people who attend twelve-step meetings were raised in very religious families. Many of these people had terrible experiences in their youth. Many LGBTQ members were ostracized by their families and the churches they grew up in. They were bullied, beaten, and some barely escaped certain death at the hands of their family and neighbors. I have met a few people who were physically and mentally abused by nuns, and some were abused by male church figures as well. So, when someone goes to an AA meeting for the first time and sees the word "God" written on the walls and in the books they're asked to read, you can only imagine that some bad feelings are going to come up to the surface.

Many people, including me, come into their first twelve-step meeting as atheists. Personally, I came into my first meetings angry at God. I hated God. By the time I entered my first AA meeting, I had already been sober for eight years. But when I entered a noon men's meeting at Portland's Alano Club in 2009, I was suicidal and just wanted everything to stop. I had no idea that twelve-step meetings were going to help me. I had already tried everything else available to someone suffering from mental illness. AA was the last stop for me.

I mentioned earlier that for the first few years I remained an atheist. I would say the word "God" in meetings, but it didn't mean anything to me. My sponsor never pushed the God thing on me. As long as I went to meetings, read the literature, and stayed honest with him, we were good. Eventually, I started asking my sponsor about his connection to God, and he always talked about his HP, or higher power. My sponsor seemed to have a connection to his higher power as if his higher power was his friend rather than some giant old man with a white beard and a lightning bolt in one hand, always ready to throw it at you if you messed up. My sponsor always smiled as he spoke about his higher power. I was told that I had infinite options regarding my higher power. I was now able to choose what I wanted my higher power to be. This was never an option before. Once I became used to this new information, so much of the anxiety I always felt around religion and spirituality was lifted. Life was looser now.

In the beginning, my higher power was the people in my AA meetings. The AA community as a whole gave me direction. A handful of years went by, and my relationship with my higher power changed. It became a bit more intimate. I started talking to God while praying or meditating in my room. I had conversations with my higher power while sitting in the steam room or sauna. Of course, I would do this if I were alone. I wouldn't have conversations with God if anyone was in the sauna with me. I'm not completely nuts. Over the past few years, I always feel God around me. Sometimes He is right beside me. Sometimes God fills an entire room that I happen to be in, and sometimes I feel God inside me. After my grandmother passed away in 2022, God became my best friend. I remember asking God for help the moment I found out my grandmother had died.

"God, I'm going to need your help now. I can't get through this alone. Please take good care of my grandma."

After that prayer, I knew God was number one. For a while, I tried going to church. But I never got completely comfortable at church. I went to many churches around San Francisco. The buildings were beautiful, and everyone was very nice, but for me, something was missing. During this time that I was experimenting with different churches, I had completely cut AA out of my life. That thing that was missing from my life was, of course, my AA community. I found out the hard way that I needed to be around other people who understood what being an addict in recovery was all about. Non-addicts will never understand what it's like to be in recovery from addiction. Addicts and non-addicts simply have different types of brains. And it doesn't matter how many years of sobriety I rack up; my brain will always be different from a person who doesn't have addiction issues. I'm more than happy to spend time with people who are not addicts, but I can never cut other addicts out of my life again. I will forever need that connection to live a full life.

Today, my perception of religion and spirituality has done a complete 180. When I first entered the rooms of AA, I had to develop a certain amount of patience for the Big Book thumpers, the Jesus freaks, and the people who kept bringing God and their HP into everything they talked about. I thought these people were weak and they were followers. Today, the only people I feel really sorry for are the atheists. Atheists seem to have the hardest time in twelve-step programs. If you're diabetic, would you want to work in a candy store or a donut store? That wouldn't make any sense at all. So, if you're an atheist, why would you go to AA meetings every day? That would be such a miserable time for me. But I have to remind myself that it's not for me to understand why an atheist would spend an hour of their day multiple days a week at an AA meeting. All I have to do is smile and welcome them home. So, if you're an atheist, and you think of going to a twelve-step meeting and I see you there, welcome home!

FRIENDS

If you're new to sobriety, I want you to ask yourself, "Who are my friends today?" If you do have friends, how do you spend your time together? What do you have in common? If you're new to sobriety, I assume that you used your drug(s) of choice with your friends, right? And if you're trying to get sober and stay sober, I'd like to ask this: Do your friends still drink and use? Or did they stop the same day you decided to stop? If you want to live a sober lifestyle but your friends are still doing the same running and gunning today that you used to do with them, say, last week, then how long do you think your sobriety is going to last?

Let's say you're in rehab right now. Let's say you're in rehab for the next month. Okay, so you're safe for a month. But what are you going to do when you get out of rehab? Are you going to call up your party friends and hang out? What exactly is your plan? How is this going to work? I want you to take the next five minutes and really think about this.

Okay, your five minutes are up. What answers did you come up with? When you call up the guys you have spent the last fifteen years drinking and doing coke with, what do you think is going to happen? What, you're going to meet up at some bar, catch up on how rehab was, and you're going to watch all your friends drink like crazy assholes and then bring the coke out at 10:00 pm, and you're just going to be cool? How do you see this playing out in your mind? Do you think your buddies are going to want to hang out with you out of the kindness of their hearts? Do you think they aren't going to use anything when you're around? How long do you think you're going to last out there with these virgin bubble-head thoughts in your mind?

The truth is that one of two things is going to happen: 1) You keep the same friends that you used to party with, and you relapse and party like a rock star and eventually die. 2) You tell your friends that you can't hang out with them anymore because you want to stay sober, and hopefully, you stay sober. Those are your two options when it comes to your "friends."

If you decide to cut all your friends off, this is where twelve-step meetings are crucial. You're going to need to be around people, preferably sober people, and the best place to meet other sober people is at a twelve-step meeting. You might be asking yourself, *When should I go to a twelve-step meeting?* You should go to a meeting anytime you feel like you want to use or drink. If you have cravings all day, you should go to meetings all day. Go to meetings, raise your hand, tell people how fucked up you're feeling, and get a sponsor as soon as you can. The rest will be laid out in front of you. As a junkie who just got out of rehab, this is the best plan out there for you.

Don't worry about your friends. If you're worried about people who you used to drink and do drugs with, don't waste your time. They aren't worried about you. They're just as numb and fucked up as you were back when you were using. Remember the days when you didn't care whether you lived or died? Remember when you used to steal from your family? Yeah, your friends are probably doing the same shit right now. Those people don't have the emotional intelligence right now to worry about you. They only want you around because they're hoping that you either have drugs or money to buy drugs. So just focus on yourself. Don't worry about girlfriends, dream jobs, and fast cars. You're basically a four-year-old child who throws regular temper tantrums. You have nothing to offer anyone right now. Just be sober one day at a time. Whatever you're meant to have in the future will come to you. Don't worry about any of that material shit. The more you think about it, the longer it's going to take to come.

Look, I don't mean to be a bully here, but someone has to tell you the truth. Most likely, the only way you found a copy of this book is because you came across it at some random AA meeting or some place that was built to help keep you sober for five minutes. You were probably getting close to death's door, right? Well, this means you probably don't have any friends left. You might not have anyone left to help you. I have been there, and most people who go to rehab or twelve-step meetings have been where you are right now. You're starting over. It might seem like the end of the world, but don't worry, the world is still ticking. You just have to decide who you want to be when you enter the world. You have to accept the fact that it's going to take time for you to heal from the shitshow you have been living in. Luckily for you, we addicts are resilient motherfuckers. You're going to be just fine, assuming you make the right decisions from here on out.

Most of the things you need to do will be written in books and on walls, and people will remind you of the things you need to do that are written in books and on walls. Remember, the easiest part of recovery is not using. Not drinking and using is the easy part. It's everything else that life throws at you that is going to be the hard part. Waiting in line for anything is going to drive you fucking nuts. Going to work and being on time is a bitch. Listening to people you don't like talk might send you over the edge a few hundred times. But if you can make it to some kind of twelve-step meeting, life won't feel as impossible. The more meetings you go to, the easier life becomes. This has been my experience.

Trust me, I would rather be at an AA meeting than a work board meeting any day of the week. AA meetings make board meetings tolerable for me. And some of those twelve-step people are going to be your new friends. They're going to be the people you tell everything to. You're going to have coffee with these people. You're going to hit the gym with some of these people. If you're lucky, this will be your new life. If you can tell your old friends that you used to terrorize the world with to fuck off, you're going to be just fine.

THE IMPORTANCE OF PEOPLE WATCHING

Looking back, there's one thing I wish I had known how to do years ago. I've always liked to think that I have a keen ability to see people for what they are. I always tell people that I'm street smart. But the truth is that I'm a magnet for the crazies. Criminals, scam artists, and liars have always had a thing for me. The only reason why I'm street and people smart today is because I have been scammed so many times that it's embarrassing.

Over the years, I've voluntarily given a guy off the street $200 of my own money from an ATM because he promised to give me $500 when we got back to his place, which was just two blocks away. He needed to pay a guy waiting in a car right outside the ATM. Once I gave him the money, he ran into the car, and they took off. I have fallen for that stupid game where a guy comes up to you on a bus and pulls out three plastic bottle caps and a small marble and bets you twenty bucks you can't pick the cap that has the marble under it. I lost $300 in less than three minutes on a

Seattle public bus once when I was seventeen years old doing this. I did the same thing a few weekends later. I have been robbed by a prostitute in a cheap motel room in Reno, twice in one weekend. Different prostitutes, of course. I'm not that stupid. When I was twenty-four, I signed a fake contract with a guy who claimed to be a profile modeling agent. He ran away with $5,000 of my cash, and he was a pedophile. His best friend and business partner was the father of my manager's fifteen-year-old girlfriend. I have a hundred more stories like this, but you get the point.

The reason I'm telling you all of this is because, looking back, I could have avoided all this stupid shit if I had thought about what was being presented to me. Every time I have been scammed out of anything—money, time, or energy—the people I gave all this up to were addicts. An addict knows an addict when he sees one, but I'm extremely gullible and want to see the best in people, even when the person standing in front of me is clearly a scumbag. Scumbags always have a look to them. They even talk a certain way. They're always a little disheveled, they never have the best hygiene, they always promise you something that's too good to be true, and they're always pushy and in a hurry. For some reason, I have a hard time telling these people no. Even with years of sobriety and education on what an addict is and being an addict myself, I still find myself prey to these fuckheads.

The potential for easy money and the excitement really turned me on. The element of risk and sometimes even danger really tuned my brain up. That spike of adrenaline is what it was all about. It was never the money. It was the danger of not knowing. Losing it all or doubling my money for doing next to nothing was just so damn sexy to me. Today, I see this kind of gambling as ridiculous. I just wish my brain had operated like this back when I was sixteen years old. Hell, I wish I knew better when I was thirty.

Today, at forty-five years old, I'd say that I've become proficient at what I call people watching. One might think that people watching is something you do while sitting on a park bench or at a café while sipping a $7 coffee and eating a $15 croissant sandwich. Yes, this is also people watching. But what I'm talking about is really taking in someone while talking to them. Getting up close and personal without the other person being aware of what you're doing. Whether someone approaches you at two in the morning on a random sidewalk, you're on a first date, at a job interview, or having an argument with a friend or family member. While the person you're exchanging words with is talking, try taking everything about this person in. What is their body language saying to you? Are they stressed? Is their energy casual? Look at their teeth. Are they stained? Are their lips dry and cracking? How do they smell? What are they wearing? How fast are they talking? Is their speech pressured and causing you anxiety?

People watching when the person is just inches from your face is a whole different game than if the person is twenty-five feet away and walking by you. For years, I never really looked at what was happening when someone was talking directly to me. I never put any importance on how that person was sitting or standing. If you know what to look for, you can plainly see if the person you're talking to is lying to you or simply doesn't like you and is just tolerating your presence. Having a conversation is nothing more than a game of poker. There's almost always an element of bartering and gambling. Even if you're talking to your mom, there's more going on than talking about the weather and catching up on what your dad is doing.

We choose the people we talk to for only a few reasons. Subconsciously we're all pondering what the person we're talking to can give us. Information is always the number one thing we want from someone in a conversation. Will you go out with me? Are you hiring? Asking a barber if they have time for a walk-in. Is this house for sale? Or simply, how are you today? All communication is information exchange. I don't think I'm saying anything groundbreaking here. I just think people forget what they're doing and why they're doing it when they're talking to someone.

One thing that a lot of successful scam artists have in common is their ability to manipulate other people with their communication skills. Most successful criminals are master communicators. Everyone who has conned me out of my money did so by sweet-talking me into handing it over to them. None of them forced me to give them my money. They didn't point a gun in my face. There was no physical violence. Robbing someone without the other person knowing they're being robbed is a skill. This shit happens every day, all day, and it kind of fascinates me, to tell the truth.

When I was a little kid, my mother would ask me what I wanted to be when I grew up, and I would always tell her that I wanted to be an art thief. Naturally, at the age of five years old, crime would be the direction I would want to go. I think the addict brain is attracted to crime. Everyone I have ever met who was a junkie at one point in their life turned to some form of crime in order to afford their habit. If you get an actual job, you have to wait for at least two weeks to get paid. For a true drug addict, two weeks is bullshit. Two weeks is an eternity in junkie years. I think addicts age more like dogs. One year to an addict is more like seven years. So two weeks is like two months for an addict, and this just won't do. Crime, especially petty theft, allows you to make money immediately so you can score some heroin right now. If you drink so much that you will have seizures if you don't get the booze into your body fast enough, breaking into someone's car and taking whatever is inside is the only thing that makes sense to the addict brain.

I know I'm pushing a narrative that says that a lot of people are not to be trusted. That's a dark message, and I'm fully aware that most people who will come across this book are likely on the fragile side. I know that addicts live in a lot of fear. I did. I still do sometimes. But I would be doing you a major disservice if I were to tell you that all people are good and nothing bad is going to happen to you. If you're suffering from the disease of alcoholism and addiction, I'm pretty confident that you have already experienced some horrible things in your life. And I'm confident that some people in your life have done some shitty things to you. How else did you become an addict in the first place, right? Addicts don't become addicts by accident.

In my opinion, addiction is a disease that is caused by winning the shitty genetics lottery and by the kind of environment you grew up in. There are a lot of strange factors that go into creating an addict. Too much love, not enough love, different types of abuse, diet, sleep quality, and access to or lack thereof to all the things that human beings need to flourish in society. Addiction is complicated, and the last thing we addicts need are bad people who want to take advantage of us just because they see us as easy prey. I feel that developing the ability to read people is a skill that all addicts in recovery should learn. Addiction is a disease of false feelings and thoughts, and most of us addicts seem to have a hard time with people in general. So many of us have a hard time attracting the right people as friends, lovers, and coworkers. We have a hard time sticking up for ourselves because of our low self-esteem and lack of self-worth.

For years, I was convinced that I didn't deserve good things in my life. I didn't think I deserved to be surrounded by good people who wanted the best for me. Today, I won't accept anything less than the best when it comes to people. All of the friends that I do have kick ass. My friends come in different shapes, sizes, and backgrounds, but they all have one thing in common: they're all great people. They all have good souls, and they all want to improve themselves, which is important. I'm grateful for all the lessons I have learned from all the sick people I have come across over the years. Being taken advantage of, having things taken from me—these were all blessings in disguise for me. But I don't want to go through that shit again. Once was definitely enough.

THE AMBASSADOR OF
THE TENDERLOIN

When: 2:00 pm, 5.20.24
Where: 235 Eddy Street, the Drake Hotel
What: Interview with Richard Beal

A couple of months ago, I had an overwhelming urge to make yet another big change in my life. I knew I needed to do something, but the idea that popped into my head made me a bit nervous. It didn't make sense to me at first. Something was telling me to move back to the Tenderloin District. At the time, I felt that my writing was becoming watered down and a bit dull. I needed to spice things up. I needed to reintroduce an element of danger into my life. Fuck, man, I needed something to talk about. All of San Francisco's neighborhoods had become boring to me. Everything had become too easy. What I needed was the Tenderloin.

Of all of San Francisco's neighborhoods, the Tenderloin District is the only one that can give me an unlimited amount of inspiration. The Tenderloin is on twenty-four hours a day. The TL doesn't have an off switch, and that's what I need. I need to be around aggression. I need to see all the ugliness available to us. But even with all the horrors that the Tenderloin so graciously gives us, there are moments and corners of beauty happening as well.

The 200 block of Turk Street, which has been blocked off to cars since 2020, looks great today. Kids can safely play, there's some greenery, and the street is very clean. I didn't notice all the art galleries crammed on Geary Street until a couple of weeks ago. And then there are all the mini parks such as Urban Oasis Dog Park on Turk and Hyde, the kids' park right across from the dog park, the Tenderloin Recreation Center, Tenderloin National Forest, and Boeddeker Park and Clubhouse. I never noticed any of these things because I was so focused on all the drugs and homelessness. I always wanted to get out of the TL as fast as possible. Now that I have been back in the Tenderloin for eight weeks, I have come to realize that I'm truly in the middle of everything. I'm a seven-minute bike ride to everything I enjoy doing. Somehow, the Tenderloin has connected me to the kind of life I want to live. I decided to follow what my higher power was suggesting to me, and I'm happier than I've ever been.

A couple of weeks ago, I decided that I should reach out to people who are trying to make a difference in the Tenderloin District. One of the names that kept coming up was Richard Beal. Rather than doing a lot of research on him, I decided to reach out to him directly to see if he'd be interested in allowing me to interview him for my book. I had no idea what to expect from him, but I had a feeling it was going to be great. Right away, Richard was into it.

Four days later, I was in his office at the Drake Hotel. Meeting Richard was an experience all on its own. Richard Beal entered the building a few minutes after I did. He was wearing a burgundy red and gold pinstriped suit with a matching hat, gold chain, and gold-rimmed glasses. To top it all off, Richard had a 10,000-watt smile. He's the very definition of cool in my opinion. If I didn't know better, I would have thought I was interviewing a rock star saxophone musician rather than a guy who helps people in the Tenderloin get sober, find housing, get an education, and eventually live out their dreams as well.

Here's Richard Beal for you. I hope you learn something. I know I did.

***

Mark: "Okay, so, I'm recording now. If you're comfortable, let's talk about your childhood, what it was like growing up, and then go from there. You can start wherever you want."

Richard: "Oh yeah, Richard Beal, and I'm an addict. It feels good to be here. It feels good to be alive. It feels good to be clean. And I always say welcome to anybody that's new. Welcome to a new way of life! One day at a time. You never have to use again, no matter what. You never have to take anything outside of yourself to fix what's going on inside of yourself. Anytime you think something outside of yourself is going to fix what's going on inside of yourself, that thought is the problem. Cause I already know that the disease is centered in my thinking. Anytime I think I can get enough drugs, alcohol, sex, gambling, clothes—you know, anytime I fix on Amazon, that's my new addiction right now. Amazon! You know what I'm say'n?"

Mark: "Oh yeah, 100%!"

Richard: "The disease always manifests itself. It finds different areas to affect my life because I have that obsession and compulsion that I'm going to have for the rest of my life. I haven't taken a drink or a drug since July 18, 1995. So, in July, I'll be celebrating twenty-nine years. And it took me twelve years to get clean. I went to my first meeting in 1983, and I got clean in 1995. I started getting loaded at nine years old, man. I went into the bathroom and took a hit of that weed, and I came out twenty years later. So, I had a twenty-year run, man. But you know, by God's grace, I've been clean longer than I used. That's the story for a lot of people when they get a lot of substantial clean time: we end up being clean longer than we used.

"But the whole thing is that I always realize that I'm battling the disease of addiction every day. When people talk about recovery and relapse and how relapse is a part of recovery, well, we have a whole chapter in the basic text, and I read the basic text. I read AA books. I read a lot of different books, but I primarily do NA. We have a whole chapter in the NA book talking about relapse and recovery. You can't be in recovery and relapse at the same time. They're two different processes. You're either in one or you're in the other. If you have "RE" in front of a word, that means there's a process that's involved with it. Return, relate, recover, you know what I'm say'n? I learned all this working with sponsors, working with people who have more knowledge than I did.

"People talk about how people had to die so that I could live. I don't believe that. I believe that some people had to live so that I wouldn't die. And I truly believe that because if it wasn't for the people who were here when I got here, who were truly pioneers and had knowledge about recovery, I wouldn't be here. It was the people who were here when I came into the rooms of Alcoholics Anonymous the first time. They were loving and caring, but then I went into those programs, and they had that tag therapy going on in the '80s. That didn't work for me. I grew up in Richmond, California. So, in Richmond, I didn't know nothin' about no twelve step. I didn't know nothin' about no AA or NA. The only thing I knew about was the DA. That was the only "A" I knew about. Because where I'm from, the people who got clean either went to church or went to jail. We just didn't know anything about no AA and NA or any of that stuff back in the '80s, man. Not in Richmond.

"Back then I was hustling. My father was a hustler, and you know, people can only give you what they got. My father gave me the information that he had at the time. All he knew was how to hustle and how to pimp and do things on the street, you see. He was streetwise, you know what I mean. So, he could only give that to his kids. I took a hit of that weed at nine years old, and at twelve years old I was sell'n fifty-cent joints, five-dollar matchboxes, and three-finger lids. Man, you know what I'm say'n.?

"Every school I went to in high school I got kicked out of. I went to Harry Ells in Richmond—I got kicked out of there for gang bang'n and fight'n. I went to Kennedy in Richmond—I got kicked out of there for gang bang'n and fight'n. I graduated from Richmond high adult school at night because they said if we see you in the daytime, we're call'n the police.

"I was a character, you know, me and my brothers, because I had three older brothers, and we were all one year apart. And so, sometimes we would all end up at the same school at the same time. We were like a gang back then. Not counting my uncles, and I had some cousins that were there too. I was fighting all the time back then. You fight one, then everybody comes. And so, that's why we were all gett'n kicked out of schools all the time. So, I went through all of that, and my father was sell'n weed, and my brothers were sell'n weed, and we were all hustle'n together. I can remember go'n to the liquor store, and there were so many of us, and we would go to the back of the store and just take all the alcohol we wanted and walk out. We did that on a regular basis, you know. Nobody could stop us back then, you see. That is just the way it was, man. I didn't have respect for anybody. We were kids and we didn't care. A lot of my uncles and my father had money, and they had a little power on the street, so if someone did jack us up too hard, my father and my uncles would come back to that store owner or to somebody that was mess'n with us, and they would have a conversation with that store owner. This just gave us more power back then. We would go back to any store we wanted and take as much as we wanted.

"My oldest brother, Anthony, started shoot'n dope at like sixteen years old. He was the first one to start shoot'n drugs. And then later on, we all started shoot'n drugs and smoke'n drugs. It just got worse and worse. By the time I was eighteen years old, I was a full-blown addict. My father couldn't understand it because all he ever did was smoke weed. I never saw my father drunk, and I never saw him use any hard drugs. He used to gamble. We used to run poker games, and he would give me money to run over to the store for his friends. But when we all ended up dope fiends, it just broke his heart.

"Two of my brothers died of the disease of addiction. Since I've been clean, my mother died, my father died, and my brother next to me died. He took me to my first meeting. He had got eighteen months clean, and he took me to my first meeting in

Richmond. I can remember he was clean, and he was do'n well, and then he relapsed. And after that, it just wasn't the same. But I had been introduced into an atmosphere of recovery and the process of recovery, and I always thank my brother for that. My brother had a heart attack from smoke'n crack. He actually had a heart attack while in a residential program. My brother just couldn't get clean again, and he had his last heart attack and died of congestive heart failure. He had a pipe and stuff in his wheelchair where he died. He died with drugs in his system, you see, and he died three days before his forty-sixth birthday.

"My oldest brother—like I was say'n, he started shoot'n dope when he was sixteen. I let him come in and live with me in 2015 when I started working for Tenderloin Housing Clinic. I had an apartment in Hayward at the time. My wife of ten years had just passed away. She had a heart attack and died. She passed away in 2014. I was single for a little while back then, and I let my brother come stay with me. I found him dead in my house. He had a diabetic seizure from drinking alcohol. He couldn't stop drinking and using either. When I found him dead, his eyes were open, and foam was coming out of both sides of his mouth. That was March 1, 2017.

"My first wife—I got married in 2000. I had three and a half years clean, and she had ninety days. We all showed up in basic text blue tuxedos. And right after we got married, like thirty days later, she relapsed, man. She took my money, my jewelry, and everything else she could get her hands on. Someone told me they had seen my car in Lakeview. She took everything, man. So, we ended up getting an annulment.

"My second wife—I met her in the rooms of Narcotics Anonymous, and our clean dates were nine days apart. She got clean on July 9; I got clean on July 18. We would go all over the country sharing at NA meetings, conventions, and speaker jams. We were like the NA couple. We were on what you call the speakers circuit. She didn't go to any treatment program; she didn't do methadone. She walked into a meeting of Narcotics Anonymous in Fresno, California, and she stayed clean until the day she passed away. Nineteen years clean. She had a heart attack, and I watched her take her last breath.

"December 14, 2014, she took her very last breath. She got up and wasn't feeling well, and I said, 'I'm taking you to the hospital.' On the way to the hospital, she looked at me, and she was about to say something to me, but all she could do was take a breath. She slumped over, and she was gone.

"When I got her to the hospital, they couldn't bring her back. They told me the time of death was 7:04 am.

"She showed me that Narcotics Anonymous works. She showed me that recovery works. She didn't do any treatment. She just walked into a twelve-step meeting and stayed clean for nineteen years.

"After all that, like I said, my brother came and stayed with me for a while, and then he passed away.

And when he passed away, my stepmom at that time was sick with cancer as well. I met my third wife that way. She was a caregiver, and she was a priestess and a pastor of a church at that time. She was doing some hospice work, and she called me when my stepmother passed away. She called me, and that's how I met her. She was taking care of my stepmother in the nursing home, and when my brother passed away, we started dating. When my brother passed away, she came and cleaned him up before the mortician and everybody came to pick him up for the funeral home. Because he was so sick, the police came, looked, and just said that he died of natural causes. Because he had so many kinds of illness as a result of his addiction.

"When my stepmother passed away—she was a community activist—her funeral was packed. That was in January. Three months later, in March, we had my brother's funeral. Nobody was there but family. It was sad, man. It was empty. Because he didn't have any friends. He was mean at the end of his addiction. You know, when you're really into your addiction like that, you don't have friends. Both my brother's funeral and my stepmother's funeral were at the same location, and so you could see the difference between her life and his life.

"Soon after all that, I got married to my third wife, and we've been married now for seven years. She's not in the program. She's got her own type of program. She's the most spiritual person I know, and she knows a lot of people in recovery. Actually, she was in FA at one time, so she understands twelve-step programs, and she's a good fit for me. She makes me very happy. My point to all that is that it's been a road, man. It's a journey. It's been such an experience, man.

"In 2021, I had a brain hemorrhage, a stroke, and a seizure. My sponsees would come and pick me up. They'd drive all the way from San Jose and take me to a meeting and my appointments. They did all that type of stuff for me. I couldn't do that stuff anymore. They suspended my license because I had a seizure and a stroke. Here it is 2024, and I'm get'n around pretty good. I still use my cane. I like to have different canes for different occasions. Some days I don't need my cane, but on other days I'll be in pain. But I don't take anything. I don't take any medication for the pain. I don't have any prescribed opiates or anything like that. Every now and then, I might take ibuprofen or something like that, but I haven't had to do that for a while. I just don't take any drugs. My body is just so sensitive to that type of stuff.

"I'm diabetic. That's my biggest struggle—dealing with diabetes right now. That and dealing with the disease of addiction. I believe in doing service. I truly believe that people who do service regularly stay clean. I started working in the field of recovery when I was six months clean. At ninety days, I started volunteering at a place called the Ozanam Center, which was a detox run by Saint Vincent de Paul. I walked into that detox on July 19, 1995. That was the beginning of my journey of recovery. I started volunteering with Vicky and Rosemary, who were working there. I would work with Vicky in the kitchen, and she just took me upstairs and told me to fill out some paperwork for my first jobs. She made me a program aid at the detox center there. I remember looking at all my paperwork and my record. I had a file because I knew I had been there numerous times. I actually had fifty-three detox episodes, and fifty-two of them said detox only. I would do three to five days and just go back out there again. It's funny. I ended up working at that detox for five years.

"At the same time, I was working at Saint Anthony for five days. That was the program I went to while at the detox, and I graduated from that program. They asked me, 'Hey Richard, you got any family out there?' I said of course not. But I had four felony warrants. When I graduated from the program after six months, they broke down all my felonies to misdemeanors. When I graduated from my next program, they dismissed all the cases. Father Floyd from Saint Anthony came to court and spoke for me. As a result of all that, I don't have any felonies to this day.

"I was able to go to school and everything. As you can see, I have earned multiple degrees, certificates, and awards for all my work. I have been working in the recovery field for twenty-eight plus years now. They call my friend Del Seymour the mayor of the Tenderloin, and they call me the TL Ambassador."

***

When Richard and I took a break from the interview, he showed me all his awards and photos taken with Mayor London Breed, Del Seymour, and many others trying to make a difference in the Tenderloin District. I couldn't help but be amazed at how far Richard Beal had come in his life. So many of us dealing with our disease of addiction can only dream of getting clean once and for all. Many of us hope to find a job and finally be able to afford rent every month, but here I'm speaking to a man who has done all that and managed to create an amazing legacy for himself as well. I could feel that Richard is connected to literally thousands of people in the city of San Francisco, and it's such an honor to spend just a few minutes with him.

***

Richard: "You know, as I sit back down, I have to realize that some of the things I learned in life were a lesson. I watched a lot of people die, and I watched a lot of people learn how to get a second life. I'm grateful for the experiences that I have had—the good, the bad, the ugly, and everything in between. And you know, Mark, I think I have given you a pretty good outlook on what my life has been like over the past thirty years, and I'm grateful, man. I'm grateful for that struggle, those twelve years of struggling when I was first introduced to recovery. I call them my wilderness experience. You know, the stages of change: precontemplation, contemplation, preparation, action, maintenance, and all of that. It took eighteen months for the obsession to use to be lifted from me because I wanted to use and drink every day for the first eighteen months of my recovery. I just didn't because a guy told me I didn't have to use even if I wanted to. So, that's what I mean when I say people had to live so that I wouldn't die. Because the more I thought about using, the more I hung around people who said I didn't have to use, no matter what. I've been here, man, and I'm still here on the battlefield and still on a mission. And I'm going to be on this mission until the God of my understanding says, 'Mission complete.'"

Mark: "Yeah! That sounds good, Richard."

Richard: "So, on that note, I think I'm done."

Mark: "Thank you so much, Richard. That was perfect."

DEAR ROBBIE

When: 3:00 pm, 5.28.24
Where: Zoom
What: Interview with Robbie

I can still remember what it was like trying to find my first sponsor. I attended AA meetings for about three months before I was ready to buckle down and get a sponsor. I knew once I got one, I'd have to start working the steps, and I wasn't sure if I wanted to work the steps when I first started going to meetings. I wanted to observe people in the rooms before I gave AA a full commitment.

In the beginning, my home group was a men's noon meeting at an Alano club in Northwest Portland on 24th and Kearney. Most of the men were over fifty-five—a lot of doctors, lawyers, and guys who ran successful family construction companies. Most of the younger guys, in their late twenties and early thirties, were the sons, nephews, or friends of the older guys in the room who had thirty years of sobriety, had Ferraris parked outside, and sat in the most comfortable chairs in the room. The older guys with all the sobriety time, money, and prestige would sponsor all these specific younger guys they already knew. I started to see that the whole vibe at the noon meeting was a bit incestuous. I would call a bunch of these guys—guys who knew who I was—and I would ask them if they would sponsor me. A few of them made up some cheesy excuses about why they couldn't sponsor me, only to sponsor one of their best friends' kids a couple of weeks later. A few guys just never called me back.

Eventually, I met Robbie, who would turn out to be one of the friendliest, most positive people I would ever come across in my life. This would be one of those situations where God works in mysterious ways. I feel like I have mentioned Robbie in almost every book I have written. I have probably told the story of how I met Robbie more than once, but he is just that important to me.

While writing this chapter, I thought I should give Robbie a call since it has been at least a year since we last talked. After talking for a good twenty minutes, I had to ask Robbie if I could interview him for this book. Luckily, he said yes. When Robbie told me he was eighty-five years old, I knew I had to put him in this book because I don't know how many more conversations we have left. Robbie's health is starting to fail a bit, and from the way he talks, I'm not sure how much more time he has. Selfishly, I would like to always have something to look back on and remember him by. Let's see what Robbie has to say.

***

Robbie: "Maybe I'm saying this because I've been in the program for a while, but what I like to do is keep all negative thoughts out of my mind. That's the most important thing to me. For the past couple of years, when I first wake up in the morning, I try to fill myself with gratitude. First of all, because I'm still breathing and because I'm sober and because I've got a fantastic fucking life. I had read somewhere that if you fill yourself with gratitude, there won't be any room for anger, and there's a lot of truth in that.

"I monitor myself in the car. If I see something, like if someone pulls in front of me with their car, and if I say under my breath, that fucking asshole, I tell myself that's a character defect on my part. And I have no idea what the person is rushing for, but it's not up to me. I can only drive my car, not theirs too.

"And, you know, I can't think of any resentments that I have. I think I have gotten over all of that and pushed those out of the way. And I don't hate anyone. When I first came into AA, I hated everyone, a bunch of fucking losers is what I heard in my mind. I don't hate anyone now, not even the big 'T,' Trump. I might dislike him, but I don't hate him. And I just think that life's too short to carry around that kind of baggage. And there are people in meetings sometimes—I think that personalities are my biggest challenge. I get through that with people because I try and see their side of why they are the way they are. Sometimes it could be because they're brand new, and they're just assholes. And I'm not sure what more I can talk about other than the fact that I wouldn't trade my sobriety for anything. I wouldn't want that old life back. And I know that they always say that it's the first drink that gets you drunk, and that's very true. Because if I took a drink right now, I know it would be the end of my life because of health things, and I've been around long enough now, I would want to go back to the rooms because I figure I was going to be short-lived anyway.

"I don't know what else to say other than AA is the best program on the planet—for me, I should say. Maybe not for some other people, but for me, it's been the best program on the planet. And I still get a lot out of the meetings, the people in there, even the new people who share are my mentors in a way. And I hear stuff that I never heard before. When I first came in, the old-timers would say, you know, this is Alcoholics Anonymous, and we don't talk about drugs in here. And I thought I heard it all, but about a month ago, a guy goes, 'I smoke a lot of beer.' Nowadays, a lot of people are dual addicted. There are the pills and various kinds of drugs and alcohol. Alcohol was my main drug because it was so easy to get. Fortunately, fentanyl and meth weren't floating around in my using days, or I probably wouldn't be here today. I'm one of those guys—if more is available, I'm going to do more.

"I don't like that term 'garden-variety alcoholic.' Because I don't think anybody really is. We're all totally different. But you know, now that I think of it, it took me a while to get over the hump where I was able to be accepting and try something new to change my attitude and say I get to do that rather than I have to do that. Like with this dialysis machine I have been using. You know, that machine is a lifesaver for me because my kidneys aren't working, but the machine takes out the extra toxins that my system can't pass off. And so, I'm grateful for that. I'm not exactly ecstatic about having to do it because of the time frame, but that doesn't make any difference. It helps with my attitude and my mood by removing those toxins from my system.

"That's not very exciting, is it?"

Robbie and I both share a good laugh.

Mark: "Robbie, you're funny. I mean, yeah, if you feel like you're done, if there's anything else you want to add, great, but if you just want to keep it short and sweet, that works for me."

Robbie: "Yeah, you know, I love life now. And I'm not afraid of dying, but I'm at a point in life where I can't remember the last time I felt I was at the jumping-off place that it talks about in the book. And life is just full of all kinds of challenges. I just kind of hang in there, and the next thing you know, it's passed. And then I have those days where I have what I call gratitude attacks, and everything is just lined up, and I just can't fucking believe that I feel so good when that happens. And I call it a gratitude attack because it is. And I'm so grateful for being sober and not missing out on all the opportunities and stuff that life offers us. And I'm just so glad that I didn't do what I originally wanted to do before I got into the program, and that was to end my life. I was chicken. I couldn't use a gun or a knife. I started looking at tall buildings. And I thought, what if I change my mind on the way down? You know, you're fucked. So, it's an amazing life, Mark. You know, you mentioned you're forty-five, and I think you were about twenty-nine or thirty when I first got to know you, and you've been sober all those years, and at one point in your life, you're just going to look back on your life, and you won't be able to believe some of the things you've thought and said. I've learned to get myself out of those negative thoughts and attitudes. And I have a pretty good relationship with most people I know today. There might be some that are assholes, but they're loving assholes.

Mark: "That's funny, Robbie."

Robbie: "That's about the size of the story, Mark."

Mark: "Great! That was perfect, Robbie. Robbie, before we go, I want to say thank you for this talk and thank you for all the help you've given me over the years. You were my first sponsor, and I'm so glad we stayed in touch all these years."

Robbie: "Well, thank you for asking me to be a part of your life."

Mark: "Absolutely!"

Robbie: "All right, well, love you, man."

Mark: "Love you too, Robbie."

IT'S A FAMILY DISEASE

I just had yet another weird conversation with my mother. I let her know that I was getting close to finishing this book and I wanted to close it by interviewing her to get her perspective and experience with addiction. My mother isn't an addict. I've never seen her drunk. Every once in a while, I'd see her with a wine cooler or a glass of white wine when I was a kid. But my mother grew up in an alcoholic home. Her biological father, stepfather, most of her uncles, grandparents, cousins—you name it. So much addiction going on. I don't think my mother is able to see how bad the addiction is on her side of the family, but I can see it clearly. I know my mother thinks I'm extremely judgmental about saying these things, and I know it makes her angry, but it is what it is.

Earlier this evening, I was talking to my mother about my addiction and my behavior, but she claims that I was always a good kid and that she doesn't think I ever had a problem with drugs and alcohol. So I started giving her example after example of my addiction, but that wasn't taking us anywhere either.

Living on the streets and going to the hospital four times for overdoses isn't out of the ordinary to my mother, I guess. Having these discussions with my mother is part fascinating and part heartbreaking. I seem to have one of those mothers who blocks out the bad things, as if nothing ever happened, and if you bring them up, you're just wasting your breath. All you get is a bunch of gaslighting followed by doubt and a flood of past traumas. None of the things that I know happened when I was a kid ever happened because my mother can't remember any of it. I know there are millions of addicts in recovery going through this very thing with their parents. The whole thing is insane to me.

What I'm telling you right now is one of the reasons why twelve-step meetings will never die. Everyone experiences some form of trauma in their life, and the smart ones will always get help. As long as humans are on this planet, mental, physical, and spiritual abuse will always exist as well. Humans are messed up. Some are just more messed up than others. If we can't go to the people we should be able to trust the most, we have to go somewhere. Some of us go to therapy, some of us marry out of our problems only to repeat them with our kids, some of us get on meds or go to an AA meeting, and some of us will drink and do heavy drugs in order to forget what happened when we were kids. We all develop an escape plan. We put on armor of some kind. We go to college, get good jobs, make money, and we spend our way out of our pain. Because what's the best thing you can do when your parents can't manipulate you anymore? You learn to manipulate yourself because that's what you know best. If you come from a family drowning in a thousand forms of addiction, it only makes sense that many of us will find a way to keep that tradition going.

Today, I like to get tattoos. I'm slowly covering my entire body with beautiful tattoos. I shop at Whole Foods a few days a week and spend way too much money on food. I manically read books on the history of jazz and obsess over my weight and how I'm aging or hopefully not aging. Saunas, steam rooms, and cold plunge tubs are my new drug of choice. I tell all my friends how they can improve their lives, what to eat and what not to eat. I tell them they have to join my gym as soon as possible because they'll never be happy if they don't take off those extra ten pounds or gain a little muscle. Today, I don't drink, but I still behave like an addict on occasion. I guess I'm telling you this so you don't feel bad if you don't get your act together right away after you decide to get sober. It's going to take years to unwind all the bad behaviors and thoughts you have swirling around in your head. I wish we could go back to normal right away.

But the hard truth is that we addicts were never normal in the first place. Our brains are different from someone who isn't an addict. This different brain by no means is an excuse for our poor behavior. We don't get a pass for beating the crap out of someone because we happened to be blackout drunk. It's not okay to cheat on our partners or abuse our kids because we like vodka and cocaine too much. And this is our side of things. This is our side of the street. We need to clean our side of the street up.

If you're reading this, you probably know this by now. As you get better over time, you're going to notice some things. You're going to see how your family behaves as a group and as individuals. You might find out that your mother is a compulsive liar and your father is a bit of a pushover when it comes to your mom, so he takes out his frustration on you or another sibling. Or maybe your younger brother gets away with more than you did as a kid. Maybe he got better grades in school than you, but he knows how to lie so well that he comes off like a complete sociopath. Somehow you became the family screw-up, but everyone around you is just as messed up as you ever were. You never realized any of this because you were drunk for the past fourteen years. Your problems were louder and out in the open, so you became the scapegoat. Everyone could get away with the crap you were doing all those years because you were a walking explosion for so long. Maybe you've tried confronting your family about their behavior, but nobody knows what the heck you're talking about. You're crazy, says your entire family. You're just making stuff up. None of what you're seeing is actually happening. If you're experiencing any of this, I'm here to tell you this is all pretty normal behavior in a dysfunctional family.

Rarely is there just one sick person in a family. Usually, everybody is a little messed up. To be dysfunctional is to be human, right? Some of us just take that dysfunction to crazy levels. I'm definitely one of those people. You might be too. But the good news is there's a twelve-step program out there somewhere that was designed just for you. The reason why I'm such an advocate for twelve-step programs is because they really do help. There's hope for anyone who needs help. Alcoholics, drug addicts, prescription pill addicts, gambling addicts, shopaholics, porn addicts, food addicts, sex addicts, people with anger issues—the list is infinite these days, and there's something for everyone.

The people around you with problems might not want to get help, but that doesn't mean you can't get help. You have the freedom to become the person you want to be. Change isn't easy. It's horrifying for most of us, but it's possible. The main reason I wanted to write this book is because I want to reach anyone who's afraid and thinks there's no way out of the life they're living right now. I want these people to know that there are so many options out there. There's help you can pay for. There are doctors, therapists, hospitals, and rehabs. And there are also free options as well. All the twelve-step meetings I've mentioned throughout this book—volunteers working around the clock at Intergroup Service Offices, mental health hotlines that are open 24/7, you name it—the help is out there. And if you're in the middle of a breakdown right now, you can always call 911. Tell the person on the other end of the phone the truth. Tell them what's going on. Someone will come out to help you. If you can't stop drinking or using other substances and you think you want to take your own life, tell someone. That first conversation could be the beginning of an entirely new life.

A TALK WITH MOM

It's 4:45 pm, June 14, 2024. I just got back from a three-day visit with my mother up in Portland, Oregon. After speaking with my first sponsor, Robbie, a couple of weeks ago, I knew I needed to take a trip up to Portland and see a few people. It has been over two years since I have seen my mother, and from what Robbie was telling me, his health hasn't been the best.

Portland has changed a lot, and I don't really like the changes, to be honest. The energy that Portland used to have is gone. I couldn't help but notice how unhappy everyone looked. I walked around downtown and Northwest Portland, and so many people had such sad looks on their faces. The Covid shutdown really hurt Portland. My entire body was telling me that I needed to get out of Portland as soon as possible.

In my mind, Portland has become the West Coast's version of New Orleans. Both Portland and New Orleans have amazing food and music scenes, but that's about it. There are no good jobs in these cities. Everyone seems to work in customer service jobs, and that's about it. Everybody is a bartender or a waiter and spends all their money on rent, tattoos, and $17 sandwiches from some random upscale café that is only open for four hours a day.

Every time I go to a city like Portland, New Orleans, Minneapolis, or Austin, I feel this slight sense of being trapped. I always have an overwhelming urge to get out as soon as possible for fear of something terrible happening and being stuck there forever without any hope of ever getting out again. Liberal hipster hubs might just be the devil's latest plan to break our souls and make us give up. But I do have to remind myself that I live in San Francisco, which is America's epicenter of bad ideas and has perfected its ability to brainwash most of its citizens to believe ridiculous things—ridiculous and dangerous ideas that destroy civilizations.

Shit, man, I know I'm spewing some dark stuff, but you have to understand that I just got back from spending three days in my hometown, and it's hard to see the place you grew up in become a shell of its former self. My visit to Portland reminded me of the last time I saw my grandma Maggie before she died. When I hugged my grandmother goodbye for the last time, her body was so fragile and frail. I knew I was holding her for the last time. This is how I felt when I left Portland yesterday. Portland is dead to me in a way.

But some amazing things happened on this last visit. Reconnecting with Robbie was a blessing. Chatting over lunch, making jokes about everything and nothing. Robbie hasn't changed since I first met him back in 2009. He is still that same peppy, good-natured man he has always been, and I love that about him. I'm so glad we have stayed in touch over the years.

I also got to spend some time with my mother. We went and got some lunch in Portland's Alberta neighborhood. Yes, we got a couple of $17 sandwiches. I tried steering our conversation in the direction of talking about her experience as a mother who had a child who would become an addict and what that was like for her, but I could tell that my mother just isn't comfortable talking about this topic. Originally, my mother agreed to let me interview her for this book, but I could tell that she's not comfortable speaking about this.

In the past, I would have just kept pushing my mother into talking about it, but I decided I need to let it rest. My mother needs to believe that nothing bad ever happened. In her mind, I never became an addict. Most of the things that happened in the past never happened in my mom's head, and this is how it needs to be for her. It's not my place to force anything on her. She has been through enough, and her happy place is forgetting the bad things. Denial is where my mother prefers to live. Who am I to even think this is wrong?

I'm a recovering addict, but I know that I'm also much more than a recovering addict. And there's more to my mother than being a woman who lives in a state of denial. Maybe the peace I'm looking for in my family, especially relative to my relationship with my mother, means that I have to simply let everything and everybody be. Just let it go. Being right and trying to get everyone to see where I'm coming from is a waste of time.

My mother and I did have a few great talks. She wanted to talk about how she never wanted children or marriage. She found a way to make amends with the decisions she has made over the years. My mother loves me, my brother, and my stepfather. She has found a way to make her life work for her, and that's a lot more than most people will ever do in their lifetime.

Most of us, including myself, will spend many years fighting the natural direction of our lives. Most of us will try to be more than what we are. We will travel all over the world looking for something that we will never find. We will try to create a career and realize that it wasn't what we actually wanted. We will chase money, position, and sex. But none of it will matter, and for many of us, we will find out the truth, but it will be too late.

My mother, on the other hand, played the hand she was dealt, and she found a way to accept it. Is my mother right? Did she miss out on anything? I have no idea. All I know is that I have to let my mother be. I have to stop tricking her into conversations and situations that make her uncomfortable. Loving my mother means loving her for who she is. This might sound simple, but I have the hardest time doing that.

I always want to make little changes and improve those in my life. This is nothing more than a fool's paradise. On this last trip to Portland, I was able to love my mother unconditionally. My mother is perfect just the way she is. I want her to be happy. So no, I didn't get that magical conversation I always wanted to have with my mother. That conversation that would answer all my questions and finally allow my mother and me to have the relationship I always dreamed of having. That may never happen, and I'm okay with that. But that uncomfortable angst I have had toward my mother since I was ten years old is gone now.

My mother is a person; I'm another kind of person. We both deserve to be who we are, right? She can't change me, and I can't change her. Why is that such a bad thing? Why was it ever a thing in the first place? Well, it's not anymore. Thank you, God. I think I know what unconditional love is now.

VICTORIOUS

Throughout our lives, we will experience moments where we feel strong. Actually, let me rephrase that. Throughout my life, I have experienced moments where I have felt strong. I keep forgetting not to speak for other people. I'm currently experiencing a time when I feel good. So many things are lining up for me. Work is going great right now. I have been able to design a work environment that I enjoy. Working alone is key. Working at a slower pace is nice as well. Keeping my interactions with other people to a minimum has proven to be ideal. I no longer have the desire to be the star of the show anymore. I don't need the attention and approval of others, and it feels great. I feel much freer right now than I have over the past few years.

Recently, I decided that I would only pursue conversations with people I find appealing on some level. If I come into contact with someone I find mentally, physically, or spiritually appealing, I will approach them. I only speak to people I find unappealing if they address me directly. In a sense,

I have taken snobbery to a spiritual level. If you're not attractive in some way, easy to talk to, have an interesting talent or if you have no interest in music, film, or art, or the desire to take care of yourself, I don't really see why we need to chat. Setting this boundary has made my life much easier and more pleasant to live. The world I live in today is simply better now that I don't allow bullshit into my life.

A couple of other things that have improved my life tremendously are listening to jazz regularly and hitting my gym's ice water bath regularly. Sitting in a tub full of 45° water has basically removed 85% of my depression. It's nothing short of a fucking miracle. Will my mental health stay in a good place for a long period? I really don't know. Only time will tell. A new company is also stepping in, taking over some of the smaller buildings that I manage, and it has offered me a free apartment just four blocks from my gym. In less than a month, I will no longer be paying rent in the second most expensive city in the US.

And I will tell you right now that none of this is luck. This is all God. God has been knocking down so many doors for me lately. I have been working my ass off and praying to God all the time. I'm fully aware that I live in a dishonest world where you can't trust 95% of the people you meet, and quite frankly, I'm over it. For years, I have experienced a deep fatigue from being so disappointed in my experiences with other people. So I turn to God now. I pray throughout the day, every day, that He helps me stay focused and enjoy my life, even the shitty parts of life. I don't work for money anymore. I work for God now. I only do what works, and this is definitely working for me. Doing this has given me a kind of freedom I never knew to be possible. The money I make is just an added bonus. Money is nothing more than a tool. I don't allow tools to take hold of my life. When I understood how important God is, my life started to feel good.

Today, life isn't just something to endure until you die. This is how I felt for most of my life. This is how I felt just six months ago. Now I know why so many people suffer from addiction, depression, anxiety, and suicidal ideation. But I couldn't understand this until I went through it myself. How can anybody truly understand something and how it works until they walk through it themselves? The only reason I can talk about these things is that I have experienced everything I'm talking about. I didn't go to school and study addiction for six years and then decide to write a bunch of books on it. I didn't take a couple of classes on depression and anxiety and then write a thesis on it. And I'm not talking about suicidal ideation for the fuck of it. These topics are heavy topics, and most people don't want to think about this shit. I'm not doing this for the money. If I wrote for money, I'd probably be writing true crime novels or romance novels, which is a billion-dollar industry, by the way. I write non-fiction autobiographical books focusing on addiction, twelve-step programs, and ways to get rid of people who are toxic for you. Nobody wants to talk about any of this shit. Most of the emails I get about my work are hate mail from random people telling me I'm a judgmental piece of shit and that I should die. But I keep writing. Why? Because I have to. If I don't write, my life will fall apart. I'm not writing because I want you to like me. I'm not looking for friends here, people. I'm just trying my best to live a good life. A life that means something, anything. And if, along the way, I can help a few people get sober, stay sober, or just think about getting sober, that's even better.

I've come to the conclusion that life isn't something you can win. I'm not sure what it means to be successful anymore. Is success a feeling? Is it a measurement of how much stuff you have? Is it a big house or a beautiful centrally located loft in Manhattan? Is it being surrounded by beautiful people who have all the nice shit I just mentioned? I used to think I knew what true success meant, but I don't. I think life is just a bunch of feelings and interactions. Life is what we make of it. But even that is something I picked up from a big-budget Hollywood movie. "Life is what you make it" sounds pretty simple to me. God, Hollywood, our parents, bosses, friends, and lovers—maybe it's all the same. I just don't know. But I do know I'm not going to drink over any of it. No fucking way!

GIVE IT AWAY, GIVE IT AWAY, GIVE IT AWAY NOW!

Let's just say, for the sake of argument, that you have been sober for a while. Let's say you're one of the lucky few who has been able to work all twelve steps of your chosen twelve-step program. I know I have mentioned the importance of sponsoring people after you have worked all twelve steps. But I want to go deeper into this phase of your recovery. Why is it so important to help other people once you're healthy enough to do so? Well, I think helping other people stay sober is the most important thing you can do for your own recovery, next to staying sober yourself, of course.

In my experience, the main reason for my depression and anxiety has to do with my self-obsession. When I'm in a dark depression, all I'm doing is obsessing over myself. Many addicts will continue to obsess over themselves years after they quit drinking and using drugs. Most of us will start thinking about ourselves even more after we quit the booze and the drugs. And why do we do this?

It's simple. Now that we can't drink and use drugs, all we have is time, and our minds are not distracted by being high or drunk. When we had our drug of choice, for hours of the day, we were completely faded out of our minds. We were given a vacation from all the mental, physical, and spiritual pain we were in. But eventually the day came when the drugs and the booze stopped working. All the chaos came flooding into our lives. It was always there, but for a while, we were numb to it. But we have already covered all this, right?

So you're sober, but you're overwhelmed by all the chaos and traffic that comes with life. All the feelings you have been running from all those years are now trapped inside you with nowhere to go. You think you might be losing your mind. Sure, you're going to AA or NA meetings, you have a sponsor, and you worked all these steps that your sponsor told you to work. But you still feel like shit. You might feel a little better. You might feel a lot better, but after a while, it's just not enough, and you start getting resentful about the fact that your life is still a mess. Maybe you have been sober for six months or a year or even a few years, but you still can't get it together. What the fuck, right? And if you can't have the life you want, what's the point of all this recovery, right?

You might be one of the very lucky few who has been able to find a sense of purpose right out of the recovery gate, but for a lot of people in recovery, things don't always go smoothly. A lot of people in recovery will tread the waters of uncertainty for quite a while. I know I did. But I have also been able to discover the most common reason for all this fear, depression, anxiety, and confusion: many of us, including myself, refused to give what we had learned in our early days of recovery back to other people. I'm extremely selfish with my time. I've been this way since I was a child. I'm a very selfish person in some ways, and I discovered that the most important thing you can give to someone in a great deal of pain is your time.

I've always hated sponsoring other people. I know that most people will never get through all the steps because most people relapse. Most people will want to use you for free therapy, and a sponsor is not a therapist. I kept these resentful feelings toward the newcomer for years, and I found myself stuck in this depressed and agitated state of being. I will be completely honest with you and tell you that I have spent probably 70% of my time sober in an uncomfortable state. I got sober in 2001, and I have literally been unhappy for most of that time. I'm telling you this so that those of you who are new in recovery can avoid making the same mistake I did. If you can stay sober and work the steps, I'm begging you to start helping people as soon as you finish step twelve. This is the best thing you can do not only for yourself but for society. Just help people like your life depends on it. Because if you have an addict brain like mine, your life does depend on it. This is not only the truth but a fact as well.

Everyone says that people who go to twelve-step meetings will definitely stay sober. I agree with part of this, but going to meetings all the time is only part of staying sober. Most if not all the people I've met who eventually relapsed are those who refused to help other people. The people who always tell you that they're too busy to sponsor someone are the people who relapse. If you're an addict and you decide to create a life where you're too busy to help other people, you're fucked. I guarantee you that. You might find a way to become a multimillionaire and marry the hottest chick in town, but if you don't help someone, you will lose everything again. This is simple math in the world of a junkie.

In the world of addiction and recovery, I feel confident saying that helping someone work the twelve steps and helping them understand the twelve traditions is just as important as becoming a parent or becoming an astronaut or a Navy SEAL or a scientist who finds a cure for a deadly disease. If you can get sober and help someone else get sober and stay sober, then you have helped perform a fucking miracle. Some of the top medical professionals will spend their entire careers trying to solve the puzzle that is addiction, and they never will. The addict brain not only needs science and medical help but also a higher power.

So while medical professionals argue with each other about what addiction is, you can help someone today. You, as a recovered addict, will have a much better chance at helping someone just like you than a Harvard graduate. I'm convinced that the smartest thing a group of doctors could ever do is team up with a handful of recovered addicts and finally make an honest attempt at battling addiction head-on, but this is an entirely different topic that deserves its own dedicated book. Note to self.

I feel that I have made my point clear on the importance of giving back to other people struggling with their addiction. No matter what happens, just do what you can. Many of the people you try to help won't really want your help. But that's okay. This isn't your fault. Just go to the next person and see what happens. Eventually, you will run into someone who really wants to get sober, and you will be there to help them. You're going to meet all types of people from many different backgrounds, but you will always have one thing in common: the disease of addiction. If you're lucky, you will have a second thing in common: you're both looking for a solution.

HAIL TO THE ALL-POWERFUL
GEOGRAPHIC!!!

There are few experiences in life more exciting than moving to a new place and starting over. Whether it's a move to a new apartment in the town you live in, a move to a new city, a move from the West Coast to the East Coast or vice versa, or a move to another country, change is its own type of high. I love moving to new places. From the very moment the idea pops into my head to check out a new place, to planning where I want to move, saving money for the move, and then leaving all my shit behind and hopping on a plane and taking off—the whole process is exhilarating.

Back in 2014, when I moved from Portland, Oregon to Key West, Florida, I was out of my mind with excitement. I felt like I was on enough cocaine to kill a horse the entire flight to Key West. I was swimming in fear and anxiety. It was such a rush. When I decided to move to San Francisco from Key West, a very similar experience overcame me. Was I making the right decision? Was I crazy or just bored? What the hell was I doing? All I knew was that I had to do it. When I arrived at the San Francisco Airport at 1:00 in the morning and my uncle picked me up and took me to my little SRO apartment in San Francisco's North Beach neighborhood, I felt like my blood had been replaced with pure electricity. I had panic attacks for the first three weeks and almost called 911 a couple of times because I thought I was having a heart attack. Most people would ask, "Why in the hell would anyone do that to themselves? Why would anyone voluntarily put themselves under that kind of stress?" There's no simple answer to these questions. But one thing I have learned from every book I have ever read or movie I have ever watched is that fortune favors the bold.

I have always wanted to live an exciting and adventurous life. For me, staying in the same town I grew up in and marrying the equivalent of some kind of high school sweetheart is the very definition of hell. But I'm speaking only for myself. I have learned that we all have our own personal definitions of what success is, and how we get there is also just as personal. For years, I thought anyone who didn't want what I wanted out of life was a fool. Learning that I was wrong about this was a painful lesson and a bit of an ego buster as well.

The reason why I'm bringing up the topic of the "geographic" is because making a big move in the first year or two of your recovery can create some unforeseen problems for you. I'm not saying that you shouldn't plan a big move, but it might be smart to hold off for a while. When I first got sober, I tried moving to another city right away and had a complete meltdown. I had to go to the hospital for severe insomnia and panic attacks. Again, this is my story, but I have talked to many people in recovery who experienced the same thing I did. We all got jobs and started making money again, so we thought we were ready for that next big step. We moved into a new place and completely turned our routines inside out, which fucked us up as well.

In those first couple of recovery years, establishing a routine that works for you is one of the most important things you can do. Addicts tend to be held together by routine. Get up, take a shower, eat some food, go to work, go to an AA meeting, eat some food, and go to bed. Keeping things as simple as possible is key. I know it sounds boring, but for most of us, the only two options we have in the beginning are boring or death. The smart ones always choose boring. I'm not saying that you're going to live a boring life from here on out, but in the beginning, boring is the best decision an addict can make. Think of it as giving your soul a vacation from all the shit you put it through while in your addiction.

It took me a while before I could start traveling again. Airports, all the people, getting on planes, spending money like a lunatic, and getting used to completely new places was a lot for me to take on. In my mind, I was ready to leave Portland when I was twenty-eight years old, but my nervous system wouldn't be ready until I was thirty-four. I tried moving to a couple of new cities, but each time I had to return with my tail tucked between my legs. The combination of anxiety and depression and the fear of going broke was just too much. My mind would tell me that I was going to lose my shit and I had better leave before I did. For years, I was so ashamed of myself. I was able to quit drinking and using, but somewhere along the way, I lost my balls for a while. I remember calling my grandmother and crying to her, telling her that I was a coward and a failure. I was already in my late twenties, and I couldn't even leave the town where I grew up to find my fortune. How can anyone ever find their true self if they can't even leave the state they were born in? I was certain that I would be stuck there for the rest of my life, too afraid to even try.

I think being warned about committing to a major geographic early on in recovery is a double-edged sword. Yes, on one hand, it's smart to wait a while before moving to a new city, however close or far away it may be. But on the other hand, if you wait too long, you may be co-signing some kind of fear you have inside. Knowing when to face your fears is also key to your growth in recovery. I know a lot of intelligent and capable people in their late twenties and older who have been sober for quite some time, and they still let their parents pay their rent and their other bills. If you're thirty-something years old and your parents are still helping you financially, I hate to say it, but this is a serious problem. If you don't have any severe mental or physical issues holding you back from living a normal life and your parents are still footing the bill for you, well, you're probably suffering from some form of arrested development.

I can't count how many women I have met in AA meetings who are in their mid-thirties but talk like little girls. They seem perpetually lost and confused. And then there are the Chads who come from wealthy parents who date these grown women that are somehow stuck inside a fourteen-year-old's mind. The rooms are filled with spoiled men who never had to face any kind of consequences during their using days, and they always seem to fall in love with women their age who are looking for their next daddy to solve all their problems for them. This is called codependency, and most twelve-step recovery meetings are drowning in this problem. This is also one of the major reasons why so many people relapse. Men and women make dick and pussy their higher power, but all it does is trick you into repeating all the mistakes you have been making for the past ten years.

To all the spoiled children in recovery, how many $50,000 rehab stays are your parents going to have to fork over until you figure your shit out? How many more cars need to be destroyed? How many times are your children going to need to be taken away from you before you finally understand that you're an addict and no man or woman is going to be able to fix you? And a side note to the parents of the world's spoiled children in recovery: When are you going to stop paying for all your kids' fuckups? I know you love your addict children, but it looks like you don't know how to love your addict children the right way. Why not seek out some help for yourself? Why not talk to other parents who went through what you're going through now and ask them what they did that you didn't do?

Maybe paying your kids' bills until they decide to figure out their lives isn't the best idea. Maybe buying them a new car when they get ninety days sober isn't going to help anything. All you're doing is reinforcing shitty behavior. You're telling your addict child that they're above the law and consequences and that they're special. I have spoken to many parents of child addicts, and for some reason, most of them seem to be immune to change. Most of them seem to be hard-wired to keep doing what they have always done, just like their kids seem hard-wired to be addicts. Of course, not all parents are like this, but, sadly, it seems like most parents are. This is the reason that I thank God for AA. If there were no twelve-step meetings to attend and all we had to rely on were our parents and doctors with good intentions, I'm sure I would already be dead. I know a lot of people who feel the same way I do.

The reason I'm telling you all this is because you want to figure some of these things out before you decide to hop on a plane and fly a couple thousand miles away to start a new life. When we first get sober, many of us are complete shit shows, and flying away from our roots could very well spell the end for us. Trust me, the new life you want to live will be there tomorrow. Hell, it will be there five years from now. Before you decide to leave whatever flyover city you're currently in, I urge you to take a moment and take a deep breath. Learn how to not scream at yourself or other people. Maybe get a job and see if you can keep it for a year. Learn to meditate and pray. Maybe take a nap. All that new shit you want now that you have seventeen days sober will be there waiting for you when you're ready for it. Hold on to your dreams and never stop fighting for them. I promise, you'll have a better chance at capturing those dreams and holding on to them once you thaw out a bit.

I don't know how long it will take you to reach a place in your life where you feel comfortable and safe. It takes all of us different amounts of time to learn and to use what we have learned to improve our lives. Everybody is different. Many of us won't make it, unfortunately, but don't focus on that. You just have to stay focused and keep moving forward.

SENSEI KEN

When: 6.18.24
Where: Zoom
What: Interview with Ken

I think having heroes throughout your life is good. Mentors, people you can look up to—these people help shape who we become as adults. My stepfather was my first hero. He was a God to me when I was a child. Not being able to measure up to what he wanted from me led to my first experience with heartbreak. When I left home at fifteen, I wouldn't just embark into an abyss of freighting experiences we call life, but I would also go on a journey seeking father figures who could replace the relationship I always wanted with my stepfather. I think not connecting with my stepfather created a hole inside my soul that I'm still trying to fill.

Throughout my life, I have collected a series of father figures, mentors, and heroes. Along the way, I have run into some amazing men, and I have learned so much from them. But these men have never replaced my stepfather. In my mind, a father is a man who will always be there, no matter what. Only a father can attempt to do this. Everyone else will just be a person who will come into your life for a time, until one day that relationship ends. A teacher will come into your life, teach you some specific things, then you will sail away, leaving your teacher to take on a whole new set of students to guide for a specific time.

Later in life you may take a job and your manager may become a different kind of teacher. This manager will teach you about life in the workplace, about how to make money, and about how to become a leader at work. But eventually, you will find a better job, and that relationship will end as well. Maybe you will take an interest in church. You might be blessed with an amazing pastor who takes an interest in you, and he will teach you about God and how to best serve God. That relationship may last for years, but the pastor will never be your father.

I feel obligated to write this chapter because I have sought out father figures throughout my years in recovery with my sponsors. My first sponsor, Robbie, was like the grandfather I always wanted: very wise, funny, successful, and emotionally open. And he wanted to help make my life better. And Robbie did just that. I would learn through Robbie that there are men in the world who are emotionally intelligent and that not all men wanted to compete with me. Not all men see me as a threat. Before Robbie, that was all I ever experienced with men.

I found another AA sponsor while living in Key West, and he was also a successful older man who is very intelligent and dynamic, and I wanted to create a life like his. I have to become as successful as my first two sponsors, but I'm confident that I will reach the kind of success I want if I just keep working hard.

And then there's my current sponsor, Ken, who I have yet to meet in person, but he has been a hero of mine for many years. When I was in my mid-twenties, I watched a TV show about addiction and recovery, and Ken played a very important role on this show. He has been a hero of mine since I was twenty-six years old. I watched that show with my grandmother every week for years. I remember Ken having such a calm demeanor. I always wished I could learn from someone like Ken.

Many years later, Covid-19 shut everything down, and I came across Ken's Instagram page. I reached out to him and thanked him for helping me through my early years of sobriety. I let him know that I might not have stayed sober if it wasn't for him. We stayed in touch, passing messages back and forth. Eventually, cities around the country would start to open up. In-person AA meetings started again. My home group at the Dry Dock had in-person and Zoom meetings, and I invited Ken to share his experience, strength, and hope via Zoom on a Friday night. He agreed to share. Ken's story really hit home for me, and I reached out to him and asked if he would be my sponsor. Ken said yes, and he has been my sponsor ever since. Ken agreed to let me record his story for all of us to learn from. With that said, here's Ken.

***

Mark: "Okay, Ken, whenever you're ready, just let me know. I'm good to go."

Ken: "Okay, I'm tryin' to think of... well, I guess it's better if you don't think about it, right?"

Mark: "Exactly! Don't worry about it, Ken. You're a pro at this."

Ken: "So, what it was like? I grew up in Middletown, New York, and while I was living in Middletown, I had a healthy upbringing, meaning my mom stayed at home and took care of me and my sister. My dad was a fireman, and he also did some work as a mechanic. My dad was always working constantly. He was working to provide for us and my mom, and I was just talking to my dad recently and he said, you know, the way that they would do it was my mom would be the good cop and my dad would be the bad cop. My mom would always tell us when things got bad. She would threaten to tell my dad, so we would always use that as a meter of sorts, which would let us know when we should stop or behave. So, it was a pretty healthy upbringing.

"But when I was three or four years old, when I started developing, I was very effeminate in my mannerisms. Not in the way I spoke but in the way I didn't play sports. I didn't know how to throw a ball.

I was different from other boys in my neighborhood. So right away I would start getting picked on at school. And I think that is when I started noticing that something was different and wrong and not right with me. I started thinking, *Oh, maybe it's the family. Maybe there's something wrong with my family, and maybe I'm not supposed to be in this family.* This would go on for many years. Four years old was when I really started to notice it, going to preschool, hiding under a table when I got there because I was afraid of everybody. And right up until junior high, when I started drinking and doing drugs. And that's when I started to not care anymore, when the drinking and drugs started.

"I think that's the changing point for me. From four to fourteen, I was paralyzed with fear and in survival mode, trying to figure out how to navigate around the world without any tools. Home was safe. And you know I work in the recovery field, so I know a lot of people who have gone through all this just like we have. Most of the people that I work with grew up in an unsafe environment at home, but I had just the opposite. I had the safe environment at home and the unsafe environment when I walked out the door because of the bullies.

"When I was fourteen, I picked up drinking and smoking pot and huffing gas and the black beauties and the yellow jackets, whatever I could get my hands on. Then when I was fifteen, sixteen, it turned into acid and mescaline and other types of drugs.

I remember this one time I went into my parents' medicine cabinet because my grandmother lived with us, and I just took all of her pills. I emptied out all of her prescriptions and I put them all in a bag. I left a few, of course, so it didn't look like I was emptying them out, and I just started taking them throughout the day when I was at school just to get out of the way. I didn't realize at the time that's what I was doing. I didn't realize at the time that's why I was taking all those pills. But I didn't like the way I felt in school, so taking drugs and drinking made me feel comfortable in my own skin.

"While I was in school, I had to go to the bathroom every three minutes. I kept raising my hand to go to the bathroom, which bothered my teacher. I found out later that I'd taken a bunch of my grandmother's water pills. It wasn't the right pill to take to get out of myself, but I just took whatever was in my bag. I was like a garbage bin. I'd take anything back then.

"Going back a little bit further, the low self-esteem also kicked in when I was in the third grade because of the bullying. I couldn't concentrate with my ADHD. It wasn't diagnosed back when I was a kid, but that's pretty much what it was. But I couldn't concentrate, so I failed third grade because I couldn't read. I couldn't keep up with the other students, and that was more evidence that there was something wrong with me. And that's what it really boils down to. There's something wrong with me, I'm not like everybody else, everybody else is perfect, and there's something wrong with me. And that's really the beginning of the root of my addiction.

"When I think of addiction, that's really what I think it is. Everybody that I have ever worked with there was something within them, me included, that we say there's something wrong with us and we can't put our finger on it. A lot of people do have horrible situations, where some people have been raped or molested, or different situations where there are lots of big examples of trauma versus the competitive trauma that I had of not knowing if I'm going to survive the next day at school because I would get beat up that day. I think that's really the difference, but I hate saying that's the difference because that's what keeps a lot of people out of the program—because they think they're different. It's a different form of trauma.

"This one guy that was at one of our treatment centers made this really clicked for me. He was a white male—tall, good-looking, in great shape. And he was saying that when he grew up, he hit puberty before all of his peers, and he was really tall and lanky and dorky. So even though he grew up in an affluent neighborhood with mostly white males in the 1970s, he said that he was bullied because he was tall and lanky. You know, there's always something, like every human being in the world has some form of trauma. We all have it. It's how we deal with it. And that's the difference between us as alcoholics and addicts: we internalize it. I internalized it. And I made it my worst weapon against myself, and I just kept attacking myself over and over and over. How stupid I am, how horrible my life is, and the world would be better off if I was dead. I just had that belief until I started doing drugs and drinking.

"Then I went into the drinking, which lasted from fourteen until I got sober at twenty-six years old. So for twelve years I drank and used, and like I said, it just kept progressing. My using went from sniffing gas to alcohol to black beauties, yellow jackets to acid to mescaline to marijuana to cocaine. Some heroin. Until the bitter end, which was meth. I realized that I really liked the stimulants when I was up and running. I always felt like I was going to miss something, so I needed to go-go-go all the time. Like if I fell asleep, I was going to miss something, like the next big opportunity. Something important was going to happen. When the bars closed, I had to be there for that, and I would go to the after-party, and I just kept going. I had all these different groups of friends because I was going to miss something, I was going to miss the miracle. It's going to happen any minute, and I'm going to miss it if I go to sleep.

"I would go through all that for those twelve years that I used, all the ups and downs, getting fired from jobs and not showing up and working really hard in between and taking breaks off. I took nine months off from drinking and using once in 1986, before I got sober. I tried to do it on my own. My grandmother was dying, and I wanted to be present for that. I did really well staying off drugs and alcohol for those nine months, but then I was like, well, marijuana wasn't really the problem. It was the alcohol, the cocaine, and meth that were the issues, so I started smoking marijuana again. But I was back on meth within a month. And you know, that's pretty much the story that I hear over and over, people trying to get sober, trying many different methods of getting sober.

"I remember right when I turned twenty-six, I thought being gay was what was wrong with me. I thought I had the drugs and alcohol under control, so maybe it's because I'm gay with the religious things out there. So I joined this twelve-step program to learn how not to be gay at this religious organization. Because I knew something was wrong, I just couldn't put my finger on it. I didn't want it to be the drugs and alcohol. It's kind of like, when you do drugs and alcohol, I explain it to people like this: I was so used to, from four to fourteen, being bullied, and drugs worked for me. They were like a miracle. I was able to finally breathe and not feel like a captive animal locked up in a cage. I felt like, *Oh my God, this is what life is all about!* So, it worked for me. It works for us people in addiction. We finally don't feel the pain. Like I said, for some people it's rape, for some people it's being molested, for some people it's unhealthy environments at home. That wasn't it for me, but it's all the same in a way. We just don't feel comfortable in our skin. I didn't feel comfortable in my skin. The drinking and the drugs worked for me. So you're telling me you're going to take that way from me?

"From four to fourteen, it was horrible. I'd get on the bus, and people would pull my hat off in the winter and throw it around the bus. If I chased it, they would all laugh. If I cried, they would all laugh. It was pure misery. After ten years of being in pain, I finally found something at fourteen that helped me self-medicate, and it made me feel like I belonged in the world and everything was okay. I finally felt really good. And now you're going to tell me that drugs and alcohol are the problem? That's everything in the world that I had. It was like someone was taking away my oxygen. If you ever went scuba diving, and you're using your regulator to breathe and you're underwater and you take away the regulator, you immediately do anything to either get back on top of the water or grab that regulator and get some oxygen. That's what it's like when you're in your addiction.

"It worked for us in our survival years. It works for millions of people. It's the thing that saves our lives. It's the reason I didn't commit suicide. You know, I was so suicidal for so many years, and that's what stopped me. I had become numb. I became numb to my reality of being in pain, so I was able to survive with the drinking and drugs. I was in survival mode, but people were telling me to stop drinking and doing drugs. I was like, I can't stop. And I didn't realize it at the time, but it was just too uncomfortable for me to stop doing drugs because I would feel again. I didn't want to go back to feeling. I didn't want to go back to not surviving. I had finally learned how to survive, and going back was just too much. Taking away the crutch of the drugs was going to take me back to the raw fear I had lived with for so long before I found my medicine.

"I didn't realize it at the time, but going back to pain and fear was what was keeping me from going back to sobriety. If I could just get past the pain and fear, I knew I would have a chance at staying sober. Like I said before I quit drinking and using the first time because I wanted to be present when my grandmother died. I wanted to be there for her, so I didn't use for those nine months before she died. But then the raw emotions, without a program, without support, without therapy, without all the tools that are necessary to get me from that trauma reaction to healthy living without the substances—I think to go from being very sick to getting to a healthy place is humanly impossible without all the things I just mentioned. And, finally, it clicked when I felt enough pain. And I think this is a really key component for everybody's recovery because so many people—you know I'm known for doing interventions, you know this is what I've been doing for many, many years in my career—interventions are intrusive, interventions are punitive, interventions are a negative way to put a spotlight on someone's disease. A lot of people say they don't want to do an intervention because they don't want to be that negative thing in a sick person's life. They don't want to feel like they're exploiting the sick person because they're vulnerable. But when I look at the big picture, what it's like, what happened... I got fired from my job, my car got repossessed, I didn't know how I was going to pay my bills—those things were my rock bottom. Poverty was my bottom. The rug was being pulled from under me, so the pain of things... if all of those things didn't happen all at once the way they did, I don't think I would have gotten sober. I think I would have stayed out there until I died.

"It was the pain, the punch in the gut that made me say, *Holy shit, I gotta do something different.* And I see it all the time in my career, watching others and helping others get over that threshold. When you listen to people—what it was like, what happened, and what it's like today—when they talk about what happened, it's something traumatic. It's something painful. It isn't something where they woke up and say, *Oh my God, it's beautiful today! I'm gonna go to the beach and, you know what... I'm gonna go to a nice fancy dinner tonight, and I might even get engaged.* It wasn't any of that. It was the negative things that were happening in my life, and it's the negative things that happen in other people's lives that motivate them. And that's what their intervention was. That's what my intervention was. So that's the way people get into recovery. It's through pain.

"It isn't through happiness and joy and love, because if love stopped people from drinking and using, a family's love toward their loved ones would help the addict stop. If love alone could cure this disease, we wouldn't have this disease. Because there are a lot of people watching their loved ones die from this disease every day. Happiness doesn't cure this disease. The thing that motivates me and motivates millions of others is the pain and the discomfort that moves us forward to doing something different from the survival skills that I was using for those twelve years that I drank and used drugs.

"Actually, the survival lasted a lot longer than twelve years. As a little kid I had to come up with a lot of survival skills to manipulate and learn how to be invisible. That's why I failed third grade. All of those things that I had to learn—those survival skills had to be wiped away and I had to surrender to saying I don't know how to do this anymore and I need help. And the only way that I did that—and the only way I hear millions of others do that—is because of pain. It's almost like a beautifully orchestrated crisis that happens in our lives. If I just lost my job but I didn't lose my car and I didn't lose my apartment or if someone was paying my bills, again, I don't think I would have gotten sober. It was the combination of all of those things crashing in at one time that made me say, *Okay, I need help. And I'm willing to do this someone else's way because I've tried every other way.*

"You know, when I was eighteen years old, I went into the Air Force. I was in for about a year and half, but I got in trouble for smoking hashish in Italy. My roommate lied and he said he didn't do it, and I told them the truth and said I smoked hash. I got kicked out, and my roommate got to stay in. That was another example of the disease, the illness, another consequence. But you know that one consequence wasn't strong enough. Because I was still surviving in survival mode. I was able to put a Band-Aid on it and say, *Oh well, I can just use the skills I learned in training and get a job*. At nineteen or twenty years old, there's no way you're going to tell me that I have to do some things differently because I've been figuring things out for a long time and I'm going to figure this problem out too.

"So even though I got kicked out of the Air Force, that wasn't the combination I needed to make me change my ways. And the sad part is a lot of people get sober at nineteen, so if there were more situations added to my getting kicked out of the Air Force, maybe I would have gotten sober back then. When I got kicked out of the Air Force, my parents were gracious enough to take me back in, but maybe if my parents would have said, "We'll take you back in, but we're going to take you back in under contract. You're not going to drink and use in this house." Other things could have happened, and I'm not saying they should have done something different in order to change my sobriety date. I'm just saying that if other consequences were in place—like the doctor diversion programs, the nurse programs, the pilot programs—they have other things in place that help them keep their license, which helps them keep their jobs if they're a drug addict or alcoholic. They have to go to meetings, they have to go to therapy, there's random drug testing, there's a whole combination of things they have to do. And that combination of things could have helped my rock-bottom earlier on. Maybe I would have gotten sober earlier than twenty-six.

"When I hit my rock bottom and surrendered finally, the pain of not being able to do it my way was so intense. I finally surrendered and said, *Okay, I'll do it another way.* I was so fortunate. I got sober in 1989, and when I got sober, a lot of my friends were dying of AIDS. I was in treatment, and the real reason I went to treatment is because I wanted to figure out how to sell crystal meth better and make a profit so I wouldn't have to go to work 9:00 to 5:00. Because I hated going to work 9:00 to 5:00. That's the real reason why I went to treatment.

"While I was in treatment, I would go to the doctors with a lot of my friends as they were dying of AIDS, and I knew I was dying but I didn't know what I was dying from. I was 130 pounds and six feet tall. I was skin and bones, doing crystal meth, and I knew something wasn't right with my body. My digestive system was all messed up. I thought I might have AIDS, but I was afraid to get tested back then. So while I was in treatment, my doctor had me do an HIV test. Back then it took three days to get your test results back. They drew blood, and the results came back three days later. The doctor sat me down and he told me that I didn't have HIV, but the bad news was that I had another disease that would kill me even faster. At the time I had no idea what the doctor was going to tell me. The doctor told me that I'm a drug addict and an alcoholic, and I was going to die the same horrible death that my friends were dying of.

"Back then, my friends had to get their AZT medication underground. It wasn't even FDA approved. You had to go to different places in order to figure out how to get your medications to just stay alive, and they were in and out of hospitals, begging doctors to keep them alive. And my friends were dropping like flies, and it was beyond horrifying. It clicked for me at that moment when my doctor said that all I had to do was don't drink and use and go to meetings. And, thank God, it hit me like a two-by-four. It hit me like a brick over the head. It hit me so hard that in July it will be thirty-five years ago, and thank God I still hear that loud and clear. Because I went to a meeting yesterday, I'm going to a meeting tomorrow, I'm still working the program of recovery, and I still haven't picked up a drink or a drug in all of that time because of that shift there in that moment, when I realized what I had to do. And yet my friends were dying and pleading and doing everything their doctors were telling them to do, and they were still dying. All I had to do was follow this doctor's recommendation, and it saved my life.

"And here we are thirty-five years later. And what has happened in those thirty-five years? Nothing but miracles—that's what has happened for me. Every time I take direction like I did with that doctor instead of doing it Ken's way, another gift pops up. Like, feeling all the pain and discomfort and dealing with it head-on and walking through it and getting sober and throwing tantrums and having anger management issues and going through all of these things, all the trial and error and pushing and shoving my way through. But the one thing that never happened was me picking up a drink and a drug.

"So I went to treatment in 1989, and with twenty-three years sober, I ended up going to anger management treatment. I originally went for two weeks of inpatient treatment, but I ended up staying for eleven weeks. I did that because that's the kind of work I want to do on myself. But things wouldn't become perfect for me just because I went to a couple of treatment centers. I would do a lot of work on myself over the years. I was really enmeshed in the twelve-step program, and with ten years sober, I bought a gun to commit suicide because I knew I didn't want to drink and use anymore because I didn't want a slow death. I wanted a quick death. I didn't want to feel the pain anymore. The pain was just too intense. And I did what the program taught me, and the program says some people need outside help. So I started searching for a therapist, and I found one who helped me realize that I was in full-blown sex addiction, love addiction, and money and work addiction.

"At ten years sober, I kept thinking that my life would be better if I had the perfect relationship. So I'd be out there, I'd go to the gym every day so I could pick up any guy I wanted or go to the clubs with my shirt off dancing just trying to find "The One." I was living that type of lifestyle at ten years sober, and it was interesting because a lot of my peers in AA would go to an AA meeting, and we would all end up at a sex club. It's pretty common to switch addictions in our recovery culture, I guess you could say. In the sober recovery world, it's very common to switch addictions from other things like alcohol and drugs to sex to food to shopping to money and working. The list can go on and on.

"So, I was in full-blown love and sex addiction. I wanted to be in a relationship like my parents and like my sister and her husband and all my cousins. But I didn't have it, and I kept blaming it on being gay. I just told myself that I didn't want to go through another breakup. At forty years old, I got dumped on my birthday, and it was just too much pain, and I decided that I'd rather not live anymore. I bought that gun on the internet, and I was ready to commit suicide because of all that pain. My doctor made me realize I was in a full-blown love and sex addiction, and I decided to go celibate. I would stay celibate for a couple years, until I finally met Erik. I feel that I was able to meet Erik because I surrendered my whole life to God. I decided I didn't need to have any more sex. I had kissed enough toads, and I could live the rest of my life without any more sex. As soon as I gave up the sex and dedicated my life to God, my life would become much more sane and eventually, like I said before, I would meet Erik, and it's been twenty years.

"And then money addiction and workaholism. I would work, work, work, trying to make money. If I only had a million dollars in the bank. If I only had more money. I'm broke all the time, I can't pay my bills, I can't take living this way. Is this what life is about—suffering and struggling? That was my other addiction my therapist helped me realize. And finally, I got to a point where I was making $10 an hour and getting people into treatment because I loved my recovery. I loved helping people getting into recovery. I could pay my car payment, and I could pay my rent, and I was in a rent-controlled building in West Hollywood, so I could live here the rest of my life and never have to worry about making a lot of money or working 24/7 to make money. Once I gave up on that, I decided I could be happy the rest of my life here.

"My parents are happy. They have a really good life together, and my dad's a retired fireman and fire inspector, so I surrendered to that. And right after I surrendered, months later, Interventions opened up and started making money, but I could go back to being celibate and being broke. Because none of that money stuff was that important anymore. What is important is for me to be comfortable in my own skin. And because I surrendered to both of those, that's when those doors opened up.

"So from the time I would get sober in 1989, through all the therapy, my work in the recovery industry and meeting my partner Erik, twenty-eight years would go by. But I have to mention that my recovery keeps opening up new doors for me. My recovery never gets stale. Like, who would have ever thought, during Covid, my dreams would become my reality instead of my nightmares because of working this program? And I continue to do this deep-dive work in my life. My mom just passed away less than a month ago, and I'm getting into doing more work, more spiritual work, more connecting with God because losing my mother is the hardest thing I have ever had to walk through in my entire life. Digging down deep and doing the work.

"Every time I dig deeper, more dreams become a reality for me. And because of all this work I have done and everything I have learned, Erik and I were able to move from California to Hawaii during Covid. We'd come to Hawaii on vacation for years together. We have traveled the world together over the last twenty years. And for years Erik and I have always said that one day it would be nice to live in Hawaii. So, all of a sudden, Erik asked if I would like to take a week off during Thanksgiving and look for a house in Hawaii. Why not? We jumped on a plane, and we actually found a place in ten days. And—boom!—we have been in Hawaii for three and a half years now.

"That's what the gift of recovery is for me. I hit a wall and dig deeper. Hit a wall and dig deeper. Hit another wall and dig even deeper. And what I see a lot of people doing is that they hit a wall and they relapse. They go back to the old thing that used to work for them as a fourteen-year-old. They don't think there's another way out. And that's what breaks my heart. If they can walk through it, things will change. The fact is, we're all going to hit walls. That's what life's about—hitting walls.

"This wall of losing my mom is the worst thing ever. It was horrible when my grandmother passed in 1986 because she was like a second mom. But this one, you know having my mom for sixty-one years, my whole life, you know, I talked to her almost every single day while she was alive. She never gave up on me, ever. She never ever gave up on me. And to lose her is like—talk about a wall. It's the hardest wall I've ever crashed into. And I know it would be easy to pick up for me. She had a lot of pain meds, she died of cancer. There was a lot of Oxys and all kinds of medications there at the house. And I know that would be a temporary relief that would destroy my life. That would give me the life of living in hell instead of living in heaven.

"And I guess that's what I'll end it with. I always believed there was a heaven and hell, which kind of stopped me from doing really bad things because I never wanted to go to hell. But now, what I realize, we can create that hell here on Earth. So many of us already have in a way. We could live in heaven constantly if we dig deeper when we hit those walls we talked about. And I know it's the hardest thing to do, but I know we all have it in us to do it.

"So, Mark, I think I should close it up now. Thank you for asking me to be a part of your book. You're doing such a great thing by writing this for all the people out there looking for a new way of living."

Mark: "Okay, Ken, that was amazing! Thank you so much for doing this."

Ken: "Oh, Mark it was my pleasure. Just send me a copy when this book is out."

Mark: "You got it, Ken. Thanks again."

WRAP IT UP!

Writing this book has been both a wild ride and a true pleasure. When I first started working on it, I almost decided to scrap it and just take some time off. But when an artist takes time off, that time off could turn into a permanent halt of creativity. In my case, the possibility of writer's block for who knows how long. The first ten pages took me five and a half months to write, and somehow the rest of the book took me seven weeks. The world of art is strange. One minute you're thinking of quitting everything, and the next thing you know, a bolt of lightning hits you, and you're blessed with a whole new purpose. I have stopped trying to figure out the method behind the madness of the creative process. I'm just so happy that I'm able to do this.

This past year, I have come out of a thirteen-month retirement from Alcoholics Anonymous, lost two of my closest friends, and moved three times. Oh, and I can't forget to mention that the two years of deep depression I've been drowning in due to my grandmother's death finally broke a month and a half ago, and my mother and I were able to squash all the bad blood that has been between us for the past thirty years. Hard times mixed with a few miracles here and there. But that's basically what life is, right? Ups and downs, good news and bad news, and everything in between. None of us signed up for it, but we're the lucky ones who got the golden ticket for the golden ride.

I know I've mentioned this a few times already, but this book is for the person battling the disease of addiction. Of course, I invite anyone to read this book. Nobody is banned from any of my work. But the person I have in mind is the one trying to stay sober. The person who is afraid and convinced they are forever cursed to be alone and to eke out some kind of miserable existence. Again, you're not alone. There are so many people who want to help you. There are literally millions of human beings who have gone through exactly what you're going through right now. You feel like shit, you're broke, and you don't know where you're going to live next month, next week, or even tomorrow. So many of us have been there. I have been there more than once. But rather than create an environment where victims gather and spew their horrible pasts all over each other, we addicts have been given tools and places to go that help us learn how to live better lives.

Twelve-step meetings, literature, social events, and outside help such as therapy and medications will change our lives forever. If you're in the first days of your recovery, get ready for an amazing journey. You're about to meet some amazing people who are going to help change everything for you. You're going to learn to laugh again. You will learn to love and to be loved again. If you're able to work hard enough, everything you have ever wanted will come into your life. Maybe not at the pace you would like it to, but it will come. Just be patient, breathe, eat a sandwich, or take a nap. You have your whole life ahead of you, and that's so much more than some people have. If you ever need anything but nobody is around, just pray. God is always there. Peace, love, and happiness to you and everyone you love.

Good luck!